Amboyna by John Dryden

OR, THE CRUELTIES OF THE DUTCH TO THE ENGLISH MERCHANTS.

A TRAGEDY.

John Dryden was born on August 9th, 1631 in the village rectory of Aldwincle near Thrapston in Northamptonshire. As a boy Dryden lived in the nearby village of Titchmarsh, Northamptonshire. In 1644 he was sent to Westminster School as a King's Scholar.

Dryden obtained his BA in 1654, graduating top of the list for Trinity College, Cambridge that year.

Returning to London during The Protectorate, Dryden now obtained work with Cromwell's Secretary of State, John Thurloe.

At Cromwell's funeral on 23 November 1658 Dryden was in the company of the Puritan poets John Milton and Andrew Marvell. The setting was to be a sea change in English history. From Republic to Monarchy and from one set of lauded poets to what would soon become the Age of Dryden.

The start began later that year when Dryden published the first of his great poems, Heroic Stanzas (1658), a eulogy on Cromwell's death.

With the Restoration of the Monarchy in 1660 Dryden celebrated in verse with Astraea Redux, an authentic royalist panegyric.

With the re-opening of the theatres after the Puritan ban, Dryden began to also write plays. His first play, The Wild Gallant, appeared in 1663 but was not successful. From 1668 on he was contracted to produce three plays a year for the King's Company, in which he became a shareholder. During the 1660s and '70s, theatrical writing was his main source of income.

In 1667, he published Annus Mirabilis, a lengthy historical poem which described the English defeat of the Dutch naval fleet and the Great Fire of London in 1666. It established him as the pre-eminent poet of his generation, and was crucial in his attaining the posts of Poet Laureate (1668) and then historiographer royal (1670).

This was truly the Age of Dryden, he was the foremost English Literary figure in Poetry, Plays, translations and other forms.

In 1694 he began work on what would be his most ambitious and defining work as translator, The Works of Virgil (1697), which was published by subscription. It was a national event.

John Dryden died on May 12th, 1700, and was initially buried in St. Anne's cemetery in Soho, before being exhumed and reburied in Westminster Abbey ten days later.

Index of Contents

AMBOYNA. AN INTRODUCTION
TO THE RIGHT HONOURABLE THE LORD CLIFFORD OF CHUDLEIGH[1].
PROLOGUE
DRAMATIS PERSONÆ
SCENE—Amboyna.
AMBOYNA
ACT I
SCENE I—A Castle on the Sea.
ACT II
SCENE I
ACT III
SCENE I
SCENE II
SCENE III—The Castle
ACT IV
SCENE I—A Wood
SCENE II
SCENE III
ACT V
SCENE I—A Table Set Out
EPILOGUE
JOHN DRYDEN – A SHORT BIOGRAPHY
JOHN DRYDEN – A CONCISE BIBLIOGRAPHY

AMBOYNA. AN INTRODUCTION

The tragedy of Amboyna, as it was justly termed by the English of the seventeenth century, was of itself too dreadful to be heightened by the mimic horrors of the stage. The reader may be reminded, that by three several treaties in the years 1613, 1615, and 1619, it was agreed betwixt England and Holland, that the English should enjoy one-third of the trade of the spice islands. For this purpose, factories were established on behalf of the English East India Company at the Molucca Islands, at Banda, and at Amboyna. At the latter island the Dutch had a castle, with a garrison, both of Europeans and natives. It has been always remarked, that the Dutchman, in his eastern settlements, loses the mercantile probity of his European character, while he retains its cold-blooded phlegm and avaricious selfishness. Of this the Amboyna government gave a notable proof. About the 11th of Feb. 1622, old stile, under pretence of a plot laid between the English of the factory and some Japanese soldiers to seize the castle, the former were arrested by the Dutch, and subjected to the most horrible tortures, to extort confession of their pretended guilt. Upon some they poured water into a cloth previously secured round their necks and shoulders, until suffocation ensued; others were tortured with lighted matches, and torches applied to the most tender and sensible parts of the body. But I will not pollute my page with this monstrous and disgusting detail. Upon confessions, inconsistent with each other, with common sense and ordinary probability, extorted also by torments of the mind or body, or both, Captain Gabriel Towerson, and nine other English merchants of consideration, were executed; and, to add insult to atrocity, the bloody cloth, on which Towerson kneeled at his death, was put down to the account of the English Company. The reader may find the whole history in the second volume of Purchas's "Pilgrim." The news of this horrible massacre reached King James, while he was negociating with the Dutch concerning the assistance which they then implored against the Spaniards; and the affairs of his son-in-law, the Elector Palatine, appeared to render an union with Holland so peremptorily necessary, that the massacre of Amboyna was allowed to remain unrevenged.

But the Dutch war, which was declared in 1672, the object of which seems to have been the annihilation of the United Provinces as an independent state, a century sooner than Providence had decreed that calamitous event, met with great opposition in England, and every engine was put to work to satisfy the people of the truth of the Lord Chancellor Shaftesbury's averment, that the "States of Holland were England's eternal enemies, both by interest and inclination." Dryden, with the avowed intention of exasperating the nation against the Dutch, assumed from choice, or by command, the unpromising subject of the Amboyna massacre as the foundation of the following play. Exclusive of the horrible nature of the subject, the colours are laid on too thick to produce the desired effect. The monstrous caricatures, which are exhibited as just paintings of the Dutch character, unrelieved even by the grandeur of wickedness, and degraded into actual brutality, must have produced disgust, instead of an animated hatred and detestation. For the horrible spectacle of tortures and mangled limbs exhibited on the stage, the author might plead the custom of his age. A stage direction in Ravenscroft's alteration of "Titus Andronicus," bears, "A curtain drawn, discovers the heads and hands of Demetrius and Chiron hanging up against the wall; their bodies in chairs, in bloody linen." And in an interlude, called the "Cruelty of the Spaniards in Peru," written by D'Avenant, "a doleful pavin is played to prepare the change of the scene, which represents a dark prison at a great distance; and farther to the view are discerned racks and other engines of torment, with which the Spaniards are tormenting the natives and English mariners, who may be supposed to be lately landed there to discover the coast. Two Spaniards are likewise discovered sitting in their cloaks, and appearing more solemn in ruffs, with rapiers and daggers by their sides; the one turning a spit, while the other is basting an Indian prince, who is roasted at an artificial fire[1]." The rape of Isabinda is stated by Langbaine to have been borrowed from a novel in the Decamerone of Cinthio Giraldi.

Footnote

1. *This extraordinary kitchen scene did not escape the ridicule of the wits of that merry age.*

O greater cruelty yet,
Like a pig upon a spit;
Here lies one there, another boiled to jelly;
Just as the people stare
At an ox in the fair,
Roasted whole, with a pudding in's belly.

A little further in,
Hung a third by his chin,
And a fourth cut all in quarters.
O that Fox had now been living,
They had been sure of heaven,
Or, at the least, been some of his martyrs.

TO THE RIGHT HONOURABLE THE LORD CLIFFORD OF CHUDLEIGH[1].

MY LORD,

After so many favours, and those so great, conferred on me by your lordship these many years,—which I may call more properly one continued act of your generosity and goodness,—I know not whether I should appear either more ungrateful in my silence, or more extravagantly vain in my endeavours to acknowledge them: For, since all acknowledgements bear a face of payment, it may be thought, that I have flattered myself into an opinion of being able to return some part of my obligations to you;—the just despair of which attempt, and the due veneration I have for his person, to whom I must address, have almost driven me to receive only with a profound submission the effects of that virtue, which is never to be comprehended but by admiration; and the greatest note of admiration is silence. It is that noble passion, to which poets raise their audience in highest subjects, and they have then gained over them the greatest victory, when they are ravished into a pleasure which is not to be expressed by words. To this pitch, my lord, the sense of my gratitude had almost raised me: to receive your favours, as the Jews of old received their law, with a mute wonder; to think, that the loudness of acclamation was only the praise of men to men, and that the secret homage of the soul was a greater mark of reverence, than an outward ceremonious joy, which might be counterfeit, and must be irreverent in its tumult. Neither, my lord, have I a particular right to pay you my acknowledgements: You have been a good so universal, that almost every man in the three nations may think me injurious to his propriety, that I invade your praises, in undertaking to celebrate them alone; and that I have assumed to myself a patron, who was no more to be circumscribed than the sun and elements, which are of public benefit to human kind.

As it was much in your power to oblige all who could pretend to merit from the public, so it was more in your nature and inclination. If any went ill-satisfied from the treasury, while it was in your lordship's management, it proclaimed the want of desert, and not of friends: You distributed your master's favour with so equal hands, that justice herself could not have held the scales more even; but with that natural propensity to do good, that had that treasure been your own, your inclination to bounty must have ruined you. No man attended to be denied: No man bribed for expedition: Want and desert were pleas sufficient. By your own integrity, and your prudent choice of those whom you employed, the king gave all that he intended; and gratuities to his officers made not vain his bounty. This, my lord, you were in your public capacity of high treasurer, to which you ascended by such degrees, that your royal master saw your virtues still growing to his favours, faster than they could rise to you. Both at home and abroad, with your sword and with your counsel, you have served him with unbiassed honour, and unshaken resolution; making his greatness, and the true interest of your country, the standard and measure of your actions. Fortune may desert the wise and brave, but true virtue never will forsake itself[2]. It is the interest of the world, that virtuous men should attain to greatness, because it gives them the power of doing good: But when, by the iniquity of the times, they are brought to that extremity, that they must either quit their virtue or their fortune, they owe themselves so much, as to retire to the private exercise of their honour;—to be great within, and by the constancy of their resolutions, to teach the inferior world how they ought to judge of such principles, which are asserted with so generous and so unconstrained a trial.

But this voluntary neglect of honours has been of rare example in the world[3]: Few men have frowned first upon fortune, and precipitated themselves from the top of her wheel, before they felt at least the declination of it. We read not of many emperors like Dioclesian and Charles the Fifth, who have preferred a garden and a cloister before a crowd of followers, and the troublesome glory of an active life, which robs the possessor of his rest and quiet, to secure the safety and happiness of others. Seneca,

with the help of his philosophy, could never attain to that pitch of virtue: He only endeavoured to prevent his fall by descending first, and offered to resign that wealth which he knew he could no longer hold; he would only have made a present to his master of what he foresaw would become his prey; he strove to avoid the jealousy of a tyrant,—you dismissed yourself from the attendance and privacy of a gracious king. Our age has afforded us many examples of a contrary nature; but your lordship is the only one of this. It is easy to discover in all governments, those who wait so close on fortune, that they are never to be shaken off at any turn: Such who seem to have taken up a resolution of being great; to continue their stations on the theatre of business; to change with the scene, and shift the vizard for another part—these men condemn in their discourses that virtue which they dare not practise: But the sober part of this present age, and impartial posterity, will do right, both to your lordship and to them: And, when they read on what accounts, and with how much magnanimity, you quitted those honours, to which the highest ambition of an English subject could aspire, will apply to you, with much more reason, what the historian said of a Roman emperor, "Multi diutius imperium tenuerunt; nemo fortius reliquit."

To this retirement of your lordship, I wish I could bring a better entertainment than this play; which, though it succeeded on the stage, will scarcely bear a serious perusal; it being contrived and written in a month, the subject barren, the persons low, and the writing not heightened with many laboured scenes. The consideration of these defects ought to have prescribed more modesty to the author, than to have presented it to that person in the world for whom he has the greatest honour, and of whose patronage the best of his endeavours had been unworthy: But I had not satisfied myself in staying longer, and could never have paid the debt with a much better play. As it is, the meanness of it will shew; at least, that I pretend not by it to make any manner of return for your favours; and that I only give you a new occasion of exercising your goodness to me, in pardoning the failings and imperfections of,

MY LORD,

Your Lordship's
Most humble, most obliged,
Most obedient servant,
JOHN DRYDEN.

Footnotes

1. *Sir Thomas Clifford, just then created Lord Clifford of Chudleigh, and appointed Lord High Treasurer, was one of the six ministers, the initials of whose names furnished the word Cabal, by which their junto was distinguished. He was the most virtuous and honest of the junto, but a Catholic; and, what was then synonymous, a warm advocate for arbitrary power. He is said to have won his promotion by advising the desperate measure of shutting the Exchequer in 1671, the hint of which he is said to have stolen from Shaftesbury. This piece may have been undertaken by his command; for, even at the very time of the triple alliance, he is reported to have said, "For all this, we must have another Dutch war." Upon the defection of Lord Shaftesbury from the court party, and the passing of the test act, Lord Clifford resigned his office, retired to the country, and died in September 1673, shortly after receiving this dedication.*

2. *In this case, Dryden's praise, which did not always occur, survived the temporary occasion. Even in a little satirical effusion, he tells us,*

Clifford was fierce and brave.

Clifford had been comptroller and treasurer of the household, and one of the commissioners of the treasury; he had served in the Dutch wars.

3. Alluding to Lord Clifford's resignation of an office he could not hold without a change of religion.

PROLOGUE

This poem was written as far back as 1662, and was then termed a Satire against the Dutch.

As needy gallants in the scriveners' hands,
Court the rich knave that gripes their mortgaged lands,
The first fat buck of all the season's sent,
And keeper takes no fee in compliment:
The dotage of some Englishmen is such
To fawn on those who ruin them—the Dutch.
They shall have all, rather than make a war
With those who of the same religion are.
The Straits, the Guinea trade, the herrings too,
Nay, to keep friendship, they shall pickle you.
Some are resolved not to find out the cheat,
But, cuckold like, love him who does the feat:
What injuries soe'er upon us fall,
Yet, still, The same religion, answers all:
Religion wheedled you to civil war,
Drew English blood, and Dutchmen's now would spare:
Be gulled no longer, for you'll find it true,
They have no more religion, faith—than you;
Interest's the god they worship in their state;
And you, I take it, have not much of that.
Well, monarchies may own religion's name,
But states are atheists in their very frame.
They share a sin, and such proportions fall,
That, like a stink, 'tis nothing to them all.
How they love England, you shall see this day;
No map shews Holland truer than our play:
Their pictures and inscriptions well we know[1];
We may be bold one medal sure to show.
View then their falsehoods, rapine, cruelty;
And think what once they were, they still would be:
But hope not either language, plot, or art;
'Twas writ in haste, but with an English heart:
And least hope wit; in Dutchmen that would be
As much improper, as would honesty.

Footnote

1. Amongst the pretexts for making war on the states of Holland were alleged their striking certain satirical medals, and engraving prints in ridicule of Charles II. See his proclamation of war in 1671-2.

DRAMATIS PERSONÆ

Captain GABRIEL TOWERSON.
Mr BEAMONT, } English Merchants, his Friends.
Mr COLLINS,   }
Captain MIDDLETON, an English Sea Captain.
PEREZ, a Spanish Captain.
HARMAN Senior, Governor of Amboyna.
The Fiscal.
HARMAN Junior, Son to the Governor.
VAN HERRING, a Dutch Merchant.

ISABINDA, betrothed to TOWERSON, an Indian Lady.
JULIA, Wife to PEREZ.
An English Woman.
Page to TOWERSON.
A Skipper.
Two Dutch Merchants.

SCENE—Amboyna

AMBOYNA

ACT I

SCENE I.—A Castle on the Sea

Enter **HARMAN Senior**, the Governor, the **FISCAL**, and **VAN HERRING: GUARDS**.

FISCAL
A happy day to our noble governor.

HARMAN Senior
Morrow, Fiscal.

VAN HERRING
Did the last ships, which came from Holland to these parts, bring us no news of moment?

FISCAL
Yes, the best that ever came into Amboyna, since we set footing here; I mean as to our interest.

HARMAN Senior
I wonder much my letters then gave me so short accounts; they only said the Orange party was grown strong again, since Barnevelt had suffered.

VAN HERRING
Mine inform me farther, the price of pepper, and of other spices, was raised of late in Europe.

HARMAN Senior
I wish that news may hold; but much suspect it, while the English maintain their factories among us in Amboyna, or in the neighbouring plantations of Seran.

FISCAL
Still I have news that tickles me within; ha, ha, ha! I'faith it does, and will do you, and all our countrymen.

HARMAN Senior
Pr'ythee do not torture us, but tell it.

VAN HERRING
Whence comes this news?

FISCAL
From England.

HARMAN Senior
Is their East India fleet bound outward for these parts, or cast away, or met at sea by pirates?

FISCAL
Better, much better yet; ha, ha, ha!

HARMAN Senior
Now am I famished for my part of the laughter.

FISCAL
Then, my brave governor, if you're a true Dutchman, I'll make your fat sides heave with the conceit on't, 'till you're blown like a pair of large smith's bellows; here, look upon this paper.

HARMAN Senior [reading.]
You may remember we did endamage the English East-India Company the value of five hundred thousand pounds, all in one year; a treaty is now signed, in which the business is ta'en up for fourscore thousand.—This is news indeed: would I were upon the castle-wall, that I might throw my cap into the sea, and my gold chain after it! this is golden news, boys.

VAN HERRING

This is news would kindle a thousand bonfires, and make us piss them out again in Rhenish wine.

HARMAN Senior
Send presently to all our factories, acquaint them with these blessed tidings: If we can 'scape so cheap, 'twill be no matter what villanies henceforth we put in practice.

FISCAL
Hum! why this now gives encouragement to a certain plot, which I have been long brewing, against these skellum English. I almost have it here In pericranio, and 'tis a sound one, 'faith; no less than to cut all their throats, and seize all their effects within this island. I warrant you we may compound again.

VAN HERRING
Seizing their factories I like well enough, it has some savour in't; but for this whoreson cutting of throats, it goes a little against the grain, because 'tis so notoriously known in Christendom, that they have preserved ours from being cut by the Spaniards.

HARMAN Senior
Hang them, base English starts, let them e'en take their part of their own old proverb—Save a thief from the gallows; they would needs protect us rebels, and see what comes to themselves.

FISCAL
You're i'the right on't, noble Harman; their assistance, which was a mercy and a providence to us, shall be a judgment upon them.

VAN HERRING
A little favour would do well; though not that I would stop the current of your wit, or any other plot, to do them mischief; but they were first discoverers of this isle, first traded hither, and showed us the way.

FISCAL
I grant you that; nay more, that, by composition made after many long and tedious quarrels, they were to have a third part of the traffic, we to build forts, and they to contribute to the charge.

HARMAN Senior
Which we have so increased each year upon them, we being in power, and therefore judges of the cost, that we exact whatever we please, still more than half the charge; and on pretence of their non-payment, or the least delay, do often stop their ships, detain their goods, and drag them into prisons, while our commodities go on before, and still forestall their markets.

FISCAL
These, I confess, are pretty tricks, but will not do our business; we must ourselves be ruined at long run, if they have any trade here; I know our charge at length will eat us out: I would not let these English from this isle have cloves enough to stick an orange with, not one to throw into their bottle-ale.

HARMAN Senior
But to bring this about now, there's the cunning.

FISCAL

Let me alone awhile; I have it, as I told you, here; mean time we must put on a seeming kindness, call them our benefactors and dear brethren, pipe them within the danger of our net, and then we'll draw it o'er them: When they're in, no mercy, that's my maxim.

VAN HERRING
Nay, brother, I am not too obstinate for saving Englishmen, 'twas but a qualm of conscience, which profit will dispel: I have as true a Dutch antipathy to England, as the proudest he in Amsterdam; that's a bold word now.

HARMAN Senior
We are secure of our superiors there. Well, they may give the king of Great Britain a verbal satisfaction, and with submissive fawning promises, make shew to punish us; but interest is their god as well as ours. To that almighty, they will sacrifice a thousand English lives, and break a hundred thousand oaths, ere they will punish those that make them rich, and pull their rivals down.

[Guns go off within.

VAN HERRING
Heard you those guns?

HARMAN Senior
Most plainly.

FISCAL
The sound comes from the port; some ship arrived salutes the castle, and I hope brings more good news from Holland.

[Guns again.

HARMAN Senior
Now they answer them from the fortress.

[Enter **BEAMONT** and **COLLINS**.

VAN HERRING
Beamont and Collins, English merchants both; perhaps they'll certify us.

BEAMONT
Captain Harman van Spelt, good day to you.

HARMAN Senior
Dear, kind Mr Beamont, a thousand and a thousand good days to you, and all our friends the English.

FISCAL
Came you from the port, gentlemen?

COLLINS
We did; and saw arrive, our honest, and our gallant countryman, brave captain Gabriel Towerson.

BEAMONT
Sent to these parts from our employers of the East India company in England, as general of the voyage.

FISCAL
Is the brave Towerson returned?

COLLINS
The same, sir.

HARMAN Senior
He shall be nobly welcome. He has already spent twelve years upon, or near, these rich Molucca isles, and home returned with honour and great wealth.

FISCAL
The devil give him joy of both, or I will for him.   [Aside.

BEAMONT
He's my particular friend; I lived with him, both at Tencrate, Tydore, and at Seran.

VAN HERRING
Did he not leave a mistress in these parts, a native of this island of Amboyna?

COLLINS
He did; I think they call her Isabinda, who received baptism for his sake, before he hence departed.

HARMAN Senior
'Tis much against the will of all her friends, she loves your countryman, but they are not disposers of her person; she's beauteous, rich, and young, and Towerson well deserves her.

BEAMONT
I think, without flattery to my friend, he does. Were I to chuse, of all mankind, a man, on whom I would rely for faith and counsel, or more, whose personal aid I would invite, in any worthy cause, to second me, it should be only Gabriel Towerson; daring he is, and thereto fortunate; yet soft, and apt to pity the distressed, and liberal to relieve them: I have seen him not alone to pardon foes, but by his bounty win them to his love: If he has any fault, 'tis only that to which great minds can only subject be—he thinks all honest, 'cause himself is so, and therefore none suspects.

FISCAL
I like him well for that; this fault of his great mind, as Beamont calls it, may give him cause to wish he was more wary, when it shall be too late.   [Aside.

HARMAN Senior
I was in some small hope, this ship had been of our own country, and brought back my son; for much about this season I expect him. Good-morrow, gentlemen; I go to fill a brendice to my noble captain's health, pray tell him so; the youth of our Amboyna I'll send before, to welcome him.

COLLINS

We'll stay, and meet him here.

[Exeunt **HARMAN Senior**, **FISCAL**, and **VAN HERRING**.

BEAMONT
I do not like these fleering Dutchmen, they overact their kindness.

COLLINS
I know not what to think of them; that old fat governor, Harman van Spelt, I have known long; they say he was a cooper in his country, and took the measure of his hoops for tuns by his own belly: I love him not, he makes a jest of men in misery; the first fat merry fool I ever knew, that was ill-natured.

BEAMONT
He's absolutely governed by this Fiscal, who was, as I have heard, an ignorant advocate in Rotterdam, such as in England we call a petty-fogging rogue; one that knows nothing, but the worst part of the law, its tricks and snares: I fear he hates us English mortally. Pray heaven we feel not the effects on't.

COLLINS
Neither he, nor Harman, will dare to shew their malice to us, now Towerson is come. For though, 'tis true, we have no castle here, he has an awe upon them in his worth, which they both fear and reverence.

BEAMONT
I wish it so may prove; my mind is a bad prophet to me, and what it does forbode of ill, it seldom fails to pay me. Here he comes.

COLLINS
And in his company young Harman, son to our Dutch governor. I wonder how they met.

[Enter **TOWERSON**, **HARMAN Junior**, and a **SKIPPER**.

TOWERSON [Entering, to the **SKIPPER**.]
These letters see conveyed with speed to our plantation. This to Cambello, and to Hitto this, this other to Loho. Tell them, their friends in England greet them well; and when I left them, were in perfect health.

SKIPPER
Sir, you shall be obeyed.

[Exit **SKIPPER**.

BEAMONT
I heartily rejoice that our employers have chose you for this place: a better choice they never could have made, or for themselves, or me.

COLLINS
This I am sure of, that our English factories in all these parts have wished you long the man, and none could be so welcome to their hearts.

HARMAN Junior
And let me speak for my countrymen, the Dutch; I have heard my father say, he's your sworn brother: And this late accident at sea, when you relieved me from the pirates, and brought my ship in safety off, I hope will well secure you of our gratitude.

TOWERSON
You over-rate a little courtesy: In your deliverance I did no more, than what I had myself from you expected: The common ties of our religion, and those, yet more particular, of peace and strict commerce betwixt us and your nation, exacted all I did, or could have done.
[To **BEAMONT**.] For you, my friend, let me ne'er breathe our English air again, but I more joy to see you, than myself to have escaped the storm that tossed me long, doubling the Cape, and all the sultry heats, in passing twice the Line: For now I have you here, methinks this happiness should not be bought at a less price.

HARMAN Junior
I'll leave you with your friends; my duty binds me to hasten to receive a father's blessing.

[Exit **HARMAN Junior**.

BEAMONT
You are so much a friend, that I must tax you for being a slack lover. You have not yet enquired of Isabinda.

TOWERSON
No; I durst not, friend, I durst not. I love too well, and fear to know my doom; there's hope in doubt; but yet I fixed my eyes on yours, I looked with earnestness, and asked with them: If aught of ill had happened, sure I had met it there; and since, methinks, I did not, I have now recovered courage, and resolve to urge it from you.

BEAMONT
Your Isabinda then—

TOWERSON
You have said all in that, my Isabinda, if she still be so.

BEAMONT
Enjoys as much of health, as fear for you, and sorrow for your absence, would permit.

[Music within.

COLLINS
Hark, music I think approaching.

BEAMONT
'Tis from our factory; some sudden entertainment I believe, designed for your return.

[Enter **AMBOYNERS, MEN** and **WOMEN**, with Timbrels before them. A Dance.

[After the Dance,

[Enter **HARMAN Senior**, **HARMAN Junior**, **FISCAL**, and **VAN HERRING**.

HARMAN Senior [Embracing **TOWERSON**.]
O my sworn brother, my dear captain Towerson! the man whom I love better than a stiff gale, when I am becalmed at sea; to whom I have received the sacrament, never to be false-hearted.

TOWERSON
You ne'er shall have occasion on my part: The like I promise for our factories, while I continue here: This isle yields spice enough for both; and Europe, ports, and chapmen, where to vend them.

HARMAN Senior
It does, it does; we have enough, if we can be contented.

TOWERSON
And, sir, why should we not? What mean these endless jars of trading nations? 'Tis true, the world was never large enough for avarice or ambition; but those who can be pleased with moderate gain, may have the ends of nature, not to want: Nay, even its luxuries may be supplied from her o'erflowing bounties in these parts; from whence she yearly sends spices and gums, the food of heaven in sacrifice: And, besides these, her gems of the richest value, for ornament, more than necessity.

HARMAN Senior
You are i'the right; we must be very friends, i'faith we must; I have an old Dutch heart, as true and trusty as your English oak.

FISCAL
We can never forget the patronage of your Elizabeth, of famous memory; when from the yoke of Spain, and Alva's pride, her potent succours, and her well-timed bounty, freed us, and gave us credit in the world.

TOWERSON
For this we only ask a fair commerce, and friendliness of conversation here: And what our several treaties bind us to, you shall, while Towerson lives, see so performed, as fits a subject to an English king.

HARMAN Senior
Now, by my faith, you ask too little, friend; we must have more than bare commerce betwixt us: Receive me to your bosom; by this beard, I will never deceive you.

BEAMONT [Aside]
I do not like his oath, there's treachery in that Judas-coloured beard.

FISCAL
Pray use me as your servant.

VAN HERRING
And me too, captain.

TOWERSON
I receive you both as jewels, which I'll wear in either ear, and never part with you.

HARMAN Senior
I cannot do enough for him, to whom I owe my son.

HARMAN Junior
Nor I, till fortune send me such another brave occasion of fighting so for you.

HARMAN Senior
Captain, very shortly we must use your head in a certain business; ha, ha, ha, my dear captain.

FISCAL
We must use your head, indeed, sir.

TOWERSON
Sir, command me, and take it as a debt I owe your love.

HARMAN Senior
Talk not of debt, for I must have your heart.

VAN HERRING
Your heart, indeed, good captain.

HARMAN Senior
You are weary now, I know, sea-beat and weary; 'tis time we respite further ceremony; besides, I see one coming, whom I know you long to embrace, and I should be unkind to keep you from her arms.

[Enter **ISABINDA** and **JULIA**.

ISABINDA
Do I hold my love, do I embrace him after a tedious absence of three years? Are you indeed returned, are you the same? Do you still love your Isabinda? Speak before I ask you twenty questions more: For I have so much love, and so much joy, that if you don't love as well as I, I shall appear distracted.

TOWERSON
We meet then both out of ourselves, for I am nothing else but love and joy; and to take care of my discretion now, would make me much unworthy of that passion, to which you set no bounds.

ISABINDA
How could you be so long away?

TOWERSON
How can you think I was? I still was here, still with you, never absent in my mind.

HARMAN Junior [Aside.
She is a most charming creature; I wish I had not seen her.

ISABINDA
Now I shall love your God, because I see that he takes care of lovers: But, my dear Englishman, I pr'ythee let it be our last of absence; I cannot bear another parting from thee, nor promise thee to live three other years, if thou again goest hence.

TOWERSON
I never will without you.

HARMAN Senior
I said before, we should but trouble ye.

TOWERSON
You make me blush; but if you ever were a lover, sir, you will forgive a folly, which is sweet, though, I confess, 'ts much extravagant.

HARMAN Junior [Aside]
He has but too much cause for this excess of joy; oh happy, happy Englishman! but I unfortunate!

TOWERSON
Now, when you please, lead on.

HARMAN Senior
This day you shall be feasted at the castle,
Where our great guns shall loudly speak your welcome.
All signs of joy shall through the isle be shewn,
Whilst in full rummers we our friendship crown.

[Exeunt.

ACT II

SCENE I

Enter **ISABINDA**, and **HARMAN Junior**.

ISABINDA
This to me, from you, against your friend!

HARMAN Junior
Have I not eyes? are you not fair? Why does it seem so strange?

ISABINDA
Come, it is a plot betwixt you: My Englishman is jealous, and has sent you to try my faith: he might have spared the experiment, after a three years absence; that was a proof sufficient of my constancy.

HARMAN Junior
I heard him say he never had returned, but that his masters of the East India company preferred him large conditions.

ISABINDA
You do bely him basely.

HARMAN Junior
As much as I do you, in saying you are fair; or as I do myself, when I declare I die for you.

ISABINDA
If this be earnest, you have done a most unmanly and ungrateful part, to court the intended wife of him, to whom you are most obliged.

HARMAN Junior
Leave me to answer that: Assure yourself I love you violently, and, if you are wise, you will make some difference betwixt Towerson and me.

ISABINDA
Yes, I shall make a difference, but not to your advantage.

HARMAN Junior
You must, or falsify your knowledge; an Englishman, part captain, and part merchant; his nation of declining interest here: Consider this, and weigh against that fellow, not me, but any, the least and meanest Dutchman in this isle.

ISABINDA
I do not weigh by bulk: I know your countrymen have the advantage there.

HARMAN Junior
Hold back your hand, from firming of your faith; you will thank me in a little time, for staying you so kindly from embarking in his ruin.

ISABINDA
His fortune is not so contemptible as you would make it seem.

HARMAN Junior
Wait but one month for the event.

ISABINDA
I will not wait one day, though I were sure to sink with him the next: So well I love my Towerson, I will not lose another sun, for fear he should not rise to-morrow. For yourself, pray rest assured, of all mankind, you should not be my choice, after an act of such ingratitude.

HARMAN Junior
You may repent your scorn at leisure.

ISABINDA

Never, unless I married you.

[Enter **TOWERSON**.

TOWERSON
Now, my dear Isabinda, I dare pronounce myself most happy:
Since I have gained your kindred, all difficulties cease.

ISABINDA
I wish we find it so.

TOWERSON
Why, is aught happened since I saw you last? Methinks a sadness dwells upon your brow, like that I saw before my last long absence. You do not speak: My friend dumb too? Nay then, I fear some more than ordinary cause produces this.

HARMAN Junior
You have no reason, Towerson, to be sad; you are the happy man.

TOWERSON
If I have any, you must needs have some.

HARMAN Junior
No, you are loved, and I am bid despair.

TOWERSON
Time and your services will perhaps make you as happy, as I am in my Isabinda's love.

HARMAN Junior
I thought I spoke so plain, I might be understood; but since I did not, I must tell you, Towerson, I wear the title of your friend no longer, because I am your rival.

TOWERSON
Is this true, Isabinda?

ISABINDA
I should not, I confess, have told you first, because I would not give you that disquiet; but since he has, it is too sad a truth.

TOWERSON
Leave us, my dear, a little to ourselves.

ISABINDA
I fear you will quarrel, for he seemed incensed, and threatened you with ruin. [To him aside.

TOWERSON
'Tis to prevent an ill, which may be fatal to us both, that I would speak with him.

ISABINDA
Swear to me, by your love, you will not fight.

TOWERSON
Fear not, my Isabinda; things are not grown to that extremity.

ISABINDA
I leave you, but I doubt the consequence.

[Exit **ISABINDA**.

TOWERSON
I want a name to call you by; friend, you declare you are not, and to rival, I am not yet enough accustomed.

HARMAN Junior
Now I consider on it, it shall be yet in your free choice, to call me one or other; for, Towerson, I do not decline your friendship, but then yield Isabinda to me.

TOWERSON
Yield Isabinda to you?

HARMAN Junior
Yes, and preserve the blessing of my friendship; I'll make my father yours; your factories shall be no more oppressed, but thrive in all advantages with ours; your gain shall be beyond what you could hope for from the treaty: In all the traffic of these eastern parts, ye shall—

TOWERSON
Hold! you mistake me, Harman, I never gave you just occasion to think I would make merchandize of love; Isabinda, you know, is mine, contracted to me ere I went for England, and must be so till death.

HARMAN Junior
She must not, Towerson; you know you are not strongest in these parts, and it will be ill contesting with your masters.

TOWERSON
Our masters? Harman, you durst not once have named that word, in any part of Europe.

HARMAN Junior
Here I both dare and will; you have no castles in Amboyna.

TOWERSON
Though we have not, we yet have English hearts, and courages not to endure affronts.

HARMAN Junior
They may be tried.

TOWERSON

Your father sure will not maintain you in this insolence; I know he is too honest.

HARMAN Junior
Assure yourself he will espouse my quarrel.

TOWERSON
We would complain to England.

HARMAN Junior
Your countrymen have tried that course so often, methinks they should grow wiser, and desist: But now there is no need of troubling any others but ourselves; the sum of all is this, you either must resign me Isabinda, or instantly resolve to clear your title to her by your sword.

TOWERSON
I will do neither now.

HARMAN Junior
Then I'll believe you dare not fight me fairly.

TOWERSON
You know I durst have fought, though I am not vain enough to boast it, nor would upbraid you with remembrance of it.

HARMAN Junior
You destroy your benefit with rehearsal of it; but that was in a ship, backed by your men; single duel is a fairer trial of your courage.

TOWERSON
I'm not to be provoked out of my temper: Here I am a public person, entrusted by my king and my employers, and should I kill you, Harman—

HARMAN Junior
Oh never think you can, sir.

TOWERSON
I should betray my countrymen to suffer, not only worse indignities than those they have already borne, but, for aught I know, might give them up to general imprisonment, perhaps betray them to a massacre.

HARMAN Junior
These are but pitiful and weak excuses; I'll force you to confess you dare not fight; you shall have provocations.

TOWERSON
I will not stay to take them. Only this before I go; if you are truly gallant, insult not where you have power, but keep your quarrel secret; we may have time and place out of this island: Meanwhile, I go to marry Isabinda, that you shall see I dare.—No more, follow me not an inch beyond this place, no not an inch. Adieu.

[Exit **TOWERSON**.

HARMAN Junior
Thou goest to thy grave, or I to mine.

[Is going after him.

[Enter **FISCAL**.

FISCAL
Whither so fast, mynheer?

HARMAN Junior
After that English dog, whom I believe you saw.

FISCAL
Whom, Towerson?

HARMAN Junior
Yes, let me go, I'll have his blood.

FISCAL
Let me advise you first; you young men are so violently hot.

HARMAN Junior
I say I'll have his blood.

FISCAL
To have his blood is not amiss, so far I go with you; but take me with you further for the means: First, what's the injury?

HARMAN Junior
Not to detain you with a tedious story, I love his mistress, courted her, was slighted; into the heat of this he came; I offered him the best advantages he could or to himself propose, or to his nation, would he quit her love.

FISCAL
So far you are prudent, for she is exceeding rich.

HARMAN Junior
He refused all; then I threatened him with my father's power.

FISCAL
That was unwisely done; your father, underhand, may do a mischief, but it is too gross aboveboard.

HARMAN Junior
At last, nought else prevailing, I defied him to single duel; this he refused, and I believe it was fear.

FISCAL
No, no, mistake him not, it is a stout whoreson. You did ill to press him, it will not sound well in Europe; he being here a public minister, having no means of 'scaping should he kill you, besides exposing all his countrymen to a revenge.

HARMAN Junior
That's all one; I'm resolved I will pursue my course, and fight him.

FISCAL
Pursue your end, that's to enjoy the woman and her wealth; I would, like you, have Towerson despatched,—for, as I am a true Dutchman, I do hate him,—but I would convey him smoothly out of the world, and without noise; they will say we are ungrateful else in England, and barbarously cruel; now I could swallow down the thing ingratitude and the thing murder, but the names are odious.

HARMAN Junior
What would you have me do then?

FISCAL
Let him enjoy his love a little while, it will break no squares in the long run of a man's life; you shall have enough of her, and in convenient time.

HARMAN Junior
I cannot bear he should enjoy her first; no, it is determined; I will kill him bravely.

FISCAL
Ay, a right young man's bravery, that's folly: Let me alone, something I'll put in practice, to rid you of this rival ere he marries, without your once appearing in it.

HARMAN Junior
If I durst trust you now?

FISCAL
If you believe that I have wit, or love you.

HARMAN Junior
Well, sir, you have prevailed; be speedy, for once I will rely on you. Farewell.

[Exit **HARMAN Junior**.

FISCAL
This hopeful business will be quickly spoiled, if I not take exceeding care of it.—Stay,—Towerson to be killed, and privately, that must be laid down as the groundwork, for stronger reasons than a young man's passion; but who shall do it? No Englishman will, and much I fear, no Dutchman dares attempt it.

[Enter **PEREZ**.

Well said, in faith, old Devil! Let thee alone, when once a man is plotting villany, to find him a fit instrument. This Spanish captain, who commands our slaves, is bold enough, and is beside in want, and proud enough to think he merits wealth.

PEREZ
This Fiscal loves my wife; I am jealous of him, and yet must speak him fair to get my pay; O, there is the devil for a Castilian, to stoop to one of his own master's rebels, who has, or who designs to cuckold him.—[Aside.]—[To **FISCAL**.] I come to kiss your hand again, sir; six months I am in arrear; I must not starve, and Spaniards cannot beg.

FISCAL
I have been a better friend to you, than perhaps you think, captain.

PEREZ [Aside]
I fear you have indeed.

FISCAL
And faithfully solicited your business; send but your wife to-morrow morning early, the money shall be ready.

PEREZ
What if I come myself?

FISCAL
Why ye may have it, if you come yourself, captain; but in case your occasions should call you any other way, you dare trust her to receive it.

PEREZ
She has no skill in money.

FISCAL
It shall be told into her hand, or given her upon honour, in a lump: but, captain, you were saying you did want; now I should think three hundred doubloons would do you no great harm; they will serve to make you merry on the watch.

PEREZ
Must they be told into my wife's hand, too?

FISCAL
No, those you may receive yourself, if you dare merit them.

PEREZ
I am a Spaniard, sir; that implies honour: I dare all that is possible.

FISCAL
Then you dare kill a man.

PEREZ

So it be fairly.

FISCAL
But what if he will not be so civil to be killed that way? He is a sturdy fellow, I know you stout, and do not question your valour; but I would make sure work, and not endanger you, who are my friend.

PEREZ
I fear the governor will execute me.

FISCAL
The governor will thank you; 'Tis he shall be your pay-master; you shall have your pardon drawn up beforehand; and remember, no transitory sum, three hundred quadruples in your own country gold.

PEREZ
Well, name your man.

[Enter **JULIA**.

FISCAL
Your wife comes, take it in whisper. [They whisper.

JULIA
Yonder is my master, and my Dutch servant; how lovingly they talk in private! if I did not know my Don's temper to be monstrously jealous, I should think, they were driving a secret bargain for my body; but cuerpo is not to be digested by my Castilian. Mi Moher, my wife, and my mistress! he lays the emphasis on me, as if to cuckold him were a worse sin, than breaking the commandment. If my English lover, Beamont, my Dutch love, the Fiscal, and my Spanish husband, were painted in a piece, with me amongst them, they would make a pretty emblem of the two nations that cuckold his Catholic majesty in his Indies.

FISCAL
You will undertake it then?

PEREZ
I have served under Towerson as his lieutenant, served him well, and, though I say it, bravely; yet never have been rewarded, though he promised largely; 'tis resolved, I'll do it.

FISCAL
And swear secresy?

PEREZ
By this beard.

FISCAL
Go wait upon the governor from me, confer with him about it in my name, this seal will give you credit.

[Gives him his seal.

PEREZ
I go.

[Goes a step or two, while the other approaches his wife.]

What shall I be, before I come again?

[Exit.

FISCAL [To **JULIA**].
Now, my fair mistress, we shall have the opportunity which I have long desired.

PEREZ
The governor is now a-sleeping; this is his hour of afternoon's repose, I'll go when he is awake.

[Returning.

FISCAL
He slept early this afternoon; I left him newly waked.

PEREZ
Well, I go then, but with an aching heart.

[Exit.

FISCAL
So, at length he's gone.

JULIA
But you may find he was jealous, by his delay.

FISCAL
If I were as you, I would give evident proofs, should cure him of that disease for ever after.

[Enter **PEREZ** again.

PEREZ
I have considered on't, and if you would go along with me to the governor, it would do much better.

FISCAL
No, no, that would make the matter more suspicious. The devil take thee for an impertinent cuckold!
[Aside.

PEREZ
Well, I must go then.

[Exit **PEREZ**.

JULIA
Nay, there was never the like of him; but it shall not serve his turn, we'll cuckold him most furiously.

[Enter **PEREZ** again.

PEREZ
I had forgot one thing; dear sweet-heart, go home quickly, and oversee our business; it won't go forward without one of us.

FISCAL
I warrant you, take no care of your business; leave it to me, I'll put it forward in your absence: Go, go, you'll lose your opportunity; I'll be at home before you, and sup with you to-night.

PEREZ
You shall be welcome, but—

FISCAL
Three hundred quadruples.

PEREZ
That's true, but—

FISCAL
But three hundred quadruples.

PEREZ
The devil take the quadruples!

[Enter **BEAMONT**.

BEAMONT
There's my cuckold that must be, and my fellow swaggerer, the Dutchman, with my mistress: my nose is wiped to-day; I must retire, for the Spaniard is jealous of me.

PEREZ
Oh, Mr Beamont, I'm to ask a favour of you.

BEAMONT
This is unusual; pray command it, signior.

PEREZ
I am going upon urgent business; pray sup with me to-night, and, in the meantime, bear my worthy friend here company.

BEAMONT
With all my heart.

PEREZ

So, now I am secure; though I dare not trust her with one of them, I may with both; they'll hinder one another, and preserve my honour into the bargain.

[Exit.

BEAMONT
Now, Mr Fiscal, you are the happy man with the ladies, and have got the precedence of traffic here too; you've the Indies in your arms, yet I hope a poor Englishman may come in for a third part of the merchandise.

FISCAL
Oh, sir, in these commodities, here's enough for both; here's mace for you, and nutmeg for me, in the same fruit, and yet the owner has to spare for other friends too.

JULIA
My husband's plantation is like to thrive well betwixt you.

BEAMONT
Horn him; he deserves not so much happiness as he enjoys in you; he's jealous.

JULIA
'Tis no wonder if a Spaniard looks yellow.

BEAMONT
Betwixt you and me, 'tis a little kind of venture that we make, in doing this Don's drudgery for him; for the whole nation of them is generally so pocky, that 'tis no longer a disease, but a second nature in them.

FISCAL
I have heard indeed, that 'tis incorporated among them, as deeply as the Moors and Jews are; there's scarce a family, but 'tis crept into their blood, like the new Christians.

JULIA
Come, I'll have no whispering betwixt you; I know you were talking of my husband, because my nose itches.

BEAMONT
Faith, madam, I was speaking in favour of your nation: What pleasant lives I have known Spaniards to live in England.

JULIA
If you love me, let me hear a little.

BEAMONT
We observed them to have much of the nature of our flies; they buzzed abroad a month or two in the summer, would venture about dog-days to take the air in the Park, but all the winter slept like dormice; and, if they ever appeared in public after Michaelmas, their faces shewed the difference betwixt their country and ours, for they look in Spain as if they were roasted, and in England as if they were sodden.

JULIA
I'll not believe your description.

FISCAL
Yet our observations of them in Holland are not much unlike it. I've known a great Don at the Hague, with the gentleman of his horse, his major domo, and two secretaries, all dine at four tables, on the quarters of a single pullet: The victuals of the under servants were weighed out in ounces, by the Don himself; with so much garlic in the other scale: A thin slice of bacon went through the family a week together; for it was daily put into the pot for pottage; was served in the midst of the dish at dinners, and taken out and weighed by the steward, at the end of every meal, to see how much it lost; till, at length, looking at it against the sun, it appeared transparent, and then he would have whipped it up, as his own fees, at a morsel; but that his lord barred the dice, and reckoned it to him for a part of his board wages.

BEAMONT
In few words, madam, the general notion we had of them, was, that they were very frugal of their Spanish coin, and very liberal of their Neapolitan.

JULIA
I see, gentlemen, you are in the way of rallying; therefore let me be no hinderance to your sport; do as much for one another as you have done for our nation. Pray, Mynheer Fiscal, what think you of the English?

FISCAL
Oh, I have an honour for the country.

BEAMONT
I beseech you, leave your ceremony; we can hear of our faults without choler; therefore speak of us with a true Amsterdam spirit, and do not spare us.

FISCAL
Since you command me, sir, 'tis said of you, I know not how truly, that for your fishery at home, you're like dogs in the manger, you will neither manage it yourselves, nor permit your neighbours; so that for your sovereignty of the narrow seas, if the inhabitants of them, the herrings, were capable of being judges, they would certainly award it to the English, because they were then sure to live undisturbed, and quiet under you.

BEAMONT
Very good; proceed, sir.

FISCAL
'Tis true, you gave us aid in our time of need, but you paid yourselves with our cautionary towns: And, that you have since delivered them up, we can never give sufficient commendation, either to your honesty, or to your wit; for both which qualities you have purchased such an immortal fame, that all nations are instructed how to deal with you another time.

BEAMONT
A most grateful acknowledgment; sweet sir, go on.

FISCAL
For your trade abroad, if you should obtain it, you are so horribly expensive, that you would undo yourselves and all Christendom; for you would sink under your very profit, and the gains of the universal world would beggar you: You devour a voyage to the Indies, by the multitude of mouths with which you man your vessels: Providence has contrived it well, that the Indies are managed by us, an industrious and frugal people, who distribute its merchandise to the rest of Europe, and suffer it not to be consumed in England, that the other members might be starved, while you of Great Britain, as you call it, like a rickety head, would only swell and grow bigger by it.

JULIA
I have heard enough of England; have you nothing to return upon the Netherlands?

BEAMONT
Faith, very little to any purpose; he has been beforehand with us, as his countrymen are in their trade, and taken up so many vices for the use of England, that he has left almost none for the Low Countries.

JULIA
Come, a word, however.

BEAMONT
In the first place, you shewed your ambition when you began to be a state: For not being gentlemen, you have stolen the arms of the best families of Europe; and wanting a name, you made bold with the first of the divine attributes, and called yourselves the High and Mighty: though, let me tell you, that, besides the blasphemy, the title is ridiculous; for High is no more proper for the Netherlands, than Mighty is for seven little rascally provinces, no bigger in all than a shire in England. For my main theme, your ingratitude, you have in part acknowledged it, by your laughing at our easy delivery of your cautionary towns: The best is, we are used by you as well as your own princes of the house of Orange: We and they have set you up, and you undermine their power, and circumvent our trade.

FISCAL
And good reason, if our interest requires it.

BEAMONT
That leads me to your religion, which is only made up of interest: At home, you tolerate all worships in them who can pay for it; and abroad, you were lately so civil to the emperor of Pegu, as to do open sacrifice to his idols.

FISCAL
Yes, and by the same token, you English were such precise fools as to refuse it.

BEAMONT
For frugality in trading, we confess we cannot compare with you; for our merchants live like noblemen; your gentlemen, if you have any, live like boors. You traffic for all the rarities of the world, and dare use none of them yourselves; so that, in effect, you are the mill-horses of mankind, that labour only for the wretched provender you eat: A pot of butter and a pickled herring is all your riches; and, in short, you have a good title to cheat all Europe, because, in the first place, you cozen your own backs and bellies.

FISCAL
We may enjoy more whenever we please.

BEAMONT
Your liberty is a grosser cheat than any of the rest; for you are ten times more taxed than any people in Christendom: You never keep any league with foreign princes; you flatter our kings, and ruin their subjects; you never denied us satisfaction at home for injuries, nor ever gave it us abroad.

FISCAL
You must make yourselves more feared, when you expect it.

BEAMONT
And I prophecy that time will come, when some generous monarch of our island will undertake our quarrel, reassume the fishery of our seas, and make them as considerable to the English, as the Indies are to you.

FISCAL
Before that comes to pass, you may repent your over-lavish tongue.

BEAMONT
I was no more in earnest than you were.

JULIA
Pray let this go no further; my husband has invited both to supper.

BEAMONT
If you please, I'll fall to before he comes; or, at least, while he is conferring in private with the Fiscal. [Aside to her.

JULIA
Their private businesses let them agree;
The Dutch for him, the Englishman for me.

[Exeunt.

ACT III

SCENE I

Enter **PEREZ**.

PEREZ
True, the reward proposed is great enough, I want it too; besides, this Englishman has never paid me since, as his lieutenant, I served him once against the Turk at sea; yet he confessed I did my duty well, when twice I cleared our decks; he has long promised me, but what are promises to starving men? this is his house, he may walk out this morning.

[Enter a **PAGE**, and another **SERVANT**, walking by, not seeing him.

These belong to him; I'll hide till they are past.

SERVANT
He sleeps soundly for a man who is to be married when he wakes.

PAGE
He does well to take his time; for he does not know, when he's married, whether ever he shall have a sound sleep again.

SERVANT
He bid we should not wake him; but some of us, in good manners, should have staid, and not have left him quite alone.

PAGE
In good manners, I should indeed; but I'll venture a master's anger at any time for a mistress, and that's my case at present.

SERVANT
I'll tempt as great a danger as that comes to, for good old English fellowship; I am invited to a morning's draught.

PAGE
Good-morrow, brother, good-morrow; by that time you have filled your belly, and I have emptied mine, it will be time to meet at home again.

[Exeunt severally.

PEREZ
So, this makes well for my design; he's left alone, unguarded, and asleep: Satan, thou art a bounteous friend, and liberal of occasions to do mischief, my pardon I have ready, if I am taken, my money half beforehand: up, Perez, rouse thy Spanish courage up; if he should wake, I think I dare attempt him; then my revenge is nobler, and revenge, to injured men, is full as sweet as profit.

[Exit.

SCENE II

The SCENE drawn, discovers **TOWERSON** asleep on a Couch in his Night-gown. A Table by him; Pen, Ink, and Paper on it.

[Re-enter **PEREZ** with a Dagger.

PEREZ

Asleep, as I imagined, and as fast as all the plummets of eternal night were hung upon his temples. Oh that some courteous dæmon, in the other world, would let him know, 'twas Perez sent him thither! A paper by him too! He little thinks it is his testament; the last he e'er shall make: I'll read it first.

[Takes it up.]

Oh, by the inscription, 'tis a memorial of what he means to do this day:
What's here? My name in the first line! I'll read it.
[Reads.]
Memorandum, That my first action this morning shall be, to find out my true and valiant lieutenant, captain Perez; and, as a testimony of my gratitude for his honourable services, to bestow on him five hundred English pounds, making my just excuse, I had it not before within my power to reward him.

[Lays down the paper.]

And was it
then for this I sought his life? Oh base, degenerate Spaniard! Hadst thou done it, thou hadst been worse than damned: Heaven took more care of me, than I of him, to expose this paper to my timely view. Sleep on, thou honourable Englishman; I'll sooner now pierce my own breast than thine: See, he smiles too in his slumber, as if his guardian angel, in a dream, told him, he was secure: I'll give him warning though, to prevent danger from another hand.
[Writes on TOWERSON'S paper, then sticks his dagger in it.
Stick there, that when he wakens, he may know,
To his own virtue he his life does owe.

[Exit **PEREZ**.

[**TOWERSON** awakens.

TOWERSON
I have o'erslept my hour this morning, if to enjoy a pleasing dream can be to sleep too long. Methought my dear Isabinda and myself were lying in an arbour, wreathed about with myrtle and with cypress; my rival Harman, reconciled again to his friendship, strewed us with flowers, and put on each a crimson-coloured garment, in which we straightway mounted to the skies; and with us, many of my English friends, all clad in the same robes. If dreams have any meaning, sure this portends some good.—What's that I see! A dagger stuck into the paper of my memorials, and writ below—Thy virtue saved thy life! It seems some one has been within my chamber whilst I slept: Something of consequence hangs upon this accident. What, ho! who waits without? None answer me? Are ye all dead? What, ho!

[Enter **BEAMONT**.

BEAMONT
How is it, friend? I thought, entering your house, I heard you call.

TOWERSON
I did, but as it seems without effect; none of my servants are within reach of my voice.

BEAMONT

You seem amazed at somewhat?

TOWERSON
A little discomposed: read that, and see if I have no occasion; that dagger was stuck there, by him who writ it.

BEAMONT
I must confess you have too just a cause: I am myself surprised at an event so strange.

TOWERSON
I know not who can be my enemy within this island, except my rival Harman; and for him, I truly did relate what passed betwixt us yesterday.

BEAMONT
You bore yourself in that as it became you, as one who was a witness to himself of his own courage; and while, by necessary care of others, you were forced to decline fighting, shewed how much you did despise the man who sought the quarrel: 'Twas base in him, so backed as he is here, to offer it, much more to press you to it.

TOWERSON
I may find a foot of ground in Europe to tell the insulting youth, he better had provoked some other man; but sure I cannot think 'twas he who left that dagger there.

BEAMONT
No, for it seems too great a nobleness of spirit, for one like him to practise: 'Twas certainly an enemy, who came to take your sleeping life; but thus to leave unfinished the design, proclaims the act no Dutchman's.

TOWERSON
That time will best discover; I'll think no further of it.

BEAMONT
I confess you have more pleasing thoughts to employ your mind at present; I left your bride just ready for the temple, and came to call you to her.

TOWERSON
I'll straight attend you thither.

[Enter **HARMAN Senior, FISCAL,** and **VAN HERRING.**

FISCAL [To **HARMAN Senior**]
Remember, sir, what I advised you; you must seemingly make up the business.

HARMAN Senior [To **TOWERSON.**
I warrant you.—What, my brave bonny bridegroom, not yet dressed? You are a lazy lover; I must chide you.

TOWERSON

I was just preparing.

HARMAN Senior
I must prevent part of the ceremony: You thought to go to her; she is by this time at the castle, where she is invited with our common friends; for you shall give me leave, if you so please, to entertain you both.

TOWERSON
I have some reasons, why I must refuse the honour you intend me.

HARMAN Senior
You must have none: What! my old friend steal a wedding from me? In troth, you wrong our friendship.

BEAMONT [To him aside.]
Sir, go not to the castle; you cannot, in honour, accept an invitation from the father, after an affront from the son.

TOWERSON
Once more I beg your pardon, sir.

HARMAN Senior
Come, come, I know your reason of refusal, but it must not prevail: My son has been to blame; I'll not maintain him in the least neglect, which he should show to any Englishman, much less to you, the best and most esteemed of all my friends.

TOWERSON
I should be willing, sir, to think it was a young man's rashness, or perhaps the rage of a successless rival; yet he might have spared some words.

HARMAN Senior
Friend, he shall ask your pardon, or I'll no longer own him; what, ungrateful to a man, whose valour has preserved him? He shall do it, he shall indeed; I'll make you friends upon your own conditions; he's at the door, pray let him be admitted; this is a day of general jubilee.

TOWERSON
You command here, you know, sir.

FISCAL
I'll call him in; I am sure he will be proud, at any rate, to redeem your kind opinion of him.

[Exit.

[**FISCAL** re-enters, with **HARMAN Junior**.

HARMAN Junior
Sir, my father, I hope, has in part satisfied you, that what I spoke was only an effect of sudden passion, of which I am now ashamed; and desire it may be no longer lodged in your remembrance, than it is now in my intention to do you any injury.

TOWERSON
Your father may command me to more difficult employments, than to receive the friendship of a man, of whom I did not willingly embrace an ill opinion.

HARMAN Junior
Nothing henceforward shall have power to take from me that happiness, in which you are so generously pleased to reinstate me.

HARMAN Senior
Why this is as it should be; trust me, I weep for joy.

BEAMONT
Towerson is easy, and too credulous. I fear 'tis all dissembled on their parts. [Aside.

HARMAN Senior
Now set we forward to the castle; the bride is there before us.

TOWERSON
Sir, I wait you.

[Exeunt **HARMAN Senior**, **TOWERSON**, **BEAMONT** and **VAN HERRING**.

[Enter Captain **PEREZ**.

FISCAL
Now, captain, when perform you what you promised, concerning Towerson's death?

PEREZ
Never.—There, Judas, take your hire of blood again.

[Throws him a purse.

HARMAN Junior
Your reason for this sudden change?

PEREZ
I cannot own the name of man, and do it.

HARMAN Junior
Your head shall answer the neglect of what you were commanded.

PEREZ
If it must, I cannot shun my destiny.

FISCAL
Harman, you are too rash; pray hear his reasons first.

PEREZ
I have them to myself, I'll give you none.

FISCAL
None? that's hard; well, you can be secret, captain, for your own sake, I hope?

PEREZ
That I have sworn already, my oath binds me.

FISCAL
That's enough: we have now chang'd our minds, and do not wish his death,—at least as you shall know. [Aside.

PEREZ
I am glad on't, for he's a brave and worthy gentleman; I would not for the wealth of both the Indies have had his blood upon my soul to answer.

FISCAL [Aside to **HARMAN Junior**.]
I shall find a time to take back our secret from him, at the price of his life, when he least dreams of it; meantime 'tis fit we speak him fair.
[To **PEREZ**.] Captain, a reward attends you, greater than you could hope; we only meant to try your honesty. I am more than satisfied of your reasons.

PEREZ
I still shall labour to deserve your kindness in any honourable way.

[Exit **PEREZ**.

HARMAN Junior
I told you that this Spaniard had not courage enough for such an enterprise.

FISCAL
He rather had too much of honesty.

HARMAN Junior
Oh, you have ruined me; you promised me this day the death of Towerson, and now, instead of that, I see him happy! I'll go and fight him yet; I swear he never shall enjoy her.

FISCAL
He shall not, that I swear with you; but you are too rash, the business can never be done your way.

HARMAN Junior
I'll trust no other arm but my own with it.

FISCAL
Yes, mine you shall, I'll help you. This evening, as he goes from the castle, we'll find some way to meet him in the dark, and then make sure of him for getting maidenheads to-night; to-morrow I'll bestow a pill upon my Spanish Don, lest he discover what he knows.

HARMAN Junior
Give me your hand, you'll help me.

FISCAL
By all my hopes I will: in the mean time, with a feigned mirth 'tis fit we gild our faces; the truth is, that we may smile in earnest, when we look upon the Englishman, and think how we will use him.

HARMAN Junior
Agreed; come to the castle.

[Exeunt.

SCENE III.—The Castle

Enter **HARMAN Senior, TOWERSON**, and **ISABINDA, BEAMONT, COLLINS, VAN HERRING**. They seat themselves.

EPITHALAMIUM.

The day is come, I see it rise,
Betwixt the bride and bridegroom's eyes;
That golden day they wished so long,
Love picked it out amidst the throng;
He destined to himself this sun,
And took the reins, and drove him on;
In his own beams he drest him bright,
Yet bid him bring a better night.

The day you wished arrived at last,
You wish as much that it were past;
One minute more, and night will hide
The bridegroom and the blushing bride.
The virgin now to bed does go—
Take care, oh youth, she rise not so—
She pants and trembles at her doom,
And fears and wishes thou wouldst come.

The bridegroom comes, he comes apace,
With love and fury in his face;
She shrinks away, he close pursues,
And prayers and threats at once does use.
She, softly sighing, begs delay,
And with her hand puts his away;
Now out aloud for help she cries,
And now despairing shuts her eyes.

HARMAN Senior
I like this song, 'twas sprightly; it would restore me twenty years of youth, had I but such a bride.

[A Dance.

[After the Dance, enter **HARMAN Junior**, and **FISCAL**.

BEAMONT
Come, let me have the Sea-Fight; I like that better than a thousand of your wanton epithalamiums.

HARMAN Junior
He means that fight, in which he freed me from the pirates.

TOWERSON [To **BEAMONT**.
Pr'ythee, friend, oblige me, and call not for that song; 'twill breed ill blood.

BEAMONT
Pr'ythee be not scrupulous, ye fought it bravely. Young Harman is ungrateful, if he does not acknowledge it. I say, sing me the Sea-Fight.

THE SEA-FIGHT.

Who ever saw a noble sight,
That never viewed a brave sea-fight!
Hang up your bloody colours in the air,
Up with your fights, and your nettings prepare;
Your merry mates cheer, with a lusty bold spright,
Now each man his brindice, and then to the fight.
St George, St George, we cry,
The shouting Turks reply:
Oh now it begins, and the gun-room grows hot,
Ply it with culverin and with small shot;
Hark, does it not thunder? no, 'tis the guns roar,
The neighbouring billows are turned into gore;
Now each man must resolve, to die,
For here the coward cannot fly.
Drums and trumpets toll the knell,
And culverins the passing bell.
Now, now they grapple, and now board amain;
Blow up the hatches, they're off all again:
Give them a broadside, the dice run at all,
Down comes the mast and yard, and tacklings fall;
She grows giddy now, like blind Fortune's wheel,
She sinks there, she sinks, she turns up her keel.
Who ever beheld so noble a sight,
As this so brave, so bloody sea-fight!

HARMAN Junior
See the insolence of these English; they cannot do a brave action in an age, but presently they must put it into metre, to upbraid us with their benefits.

FISCAL
Let them laugh, that win at last.

[Enter **Captain MIDDLETON**, and a **WOMAN** with him, all pale and weakly, and in tattered garments.

TOWERSON
Captain Middleton, you are arrived in a good hour, to be partaker of my happiness, which is as great this day, as love and expectation can make it.

[Rising up to salute **Captain MIDDLETON**.

Captain MIDDLETON
And may it long continue so!

TOWERSON
But how happens it, that, setting out with us from England, you came not sooner hither.

Captain MIDDLETON
It seems the winds favoured you with a quicker passage; you know I lost you in a storm on the other side of the Cape, with which disabled, I was forced to put into St Helen's isle; there 'twas my fortune to preserve the life of this our countrywoman; the rest let her relate.

ISABINDA
Alas, she seems half-starved, unfit to make relations.

VAN HERRING
How the devil came she off? I know her but too well, and fear she knows me too.

TOWERSON
Pray, countrywoman, speak.

ENGLISH WOMAN
Then thus in brief; in my dear husband's company, I parted from our sweet native isle: we to Lantore were bound, with letters from the States of Holland, gained for reparation of great damages sustained by us; when, by the insulting Dutch, our countrymen, against all show of right, were dispossessed, and naked sent away from that rich island, and from Poleroon.

HARMAN Junior
Woman, you speak with too much spleen; I must not hear my countrymen affronted.

ENGLISH WOMAN
I wish they did not merit much worse of me, than I can say of them.—Well, we sailed forward with a merry gale, till near St Helen's isle we were overtaken, or rather waylaid, by a Holland vessel; the captain of which ship, whom here I see, the man who quitted us of all we had in those rich parts before, now

fearing to restore his ill-got goods, first hailed, and then invited us on board, keeping himself concealed; his base lieutenant plied all our English mariners with wine, and when in dead of night they lay secure in silent sleep, most barbarously commanded they should be thrown overboard.

FISCAL
Sir, do not hear it out.

HARMAN Junior
This is all false and scandalous.

TOWERSON
Pray, sir, attend the story.

ENGLISH WOMAN
The vessel rifled, and the rich hold rummaged, they sink it down to rights; but first I should have told you, (grief, alas, has spoiled my memory) that my dear husband, wakened at the noise, before they reached the cabin where we lay, took me all trembling with the sudden fright, and leapt into the boat; we cut the cordage, and so put out to sea, driving at mercy of the waves and wind; so scaped we in the dark. To sum up all, we got to shore, and in the mountains hid us, until the barbarous Hollanders were gone.

TOWERSON
Where is your husband, countrywoman?

ENGLISH WOMAN
Dead with grief; with these two hands I scratched him out a grave, on which I placed a cross, and every day wept o'er the ground where all my joys lay buried. The manner of my life, who can express! the fountain-water was my only drink; the crabbed juice and rhind of half-ripe lemons almost my only food, except some roots; my house, the widowed cave of some wild beast. In this sad state, I stood upon the shore, when this brave captain with his ship approached, whence holding up and waving both my hands, I stood, and by my actions begged their mercy; yet, when they nearer came, I would have fled, had I been able, lest they should have proved those murderous Dutch, I more than hunger feared.

HARMAN Junior
What say you to this accusation, Van Herring?

VAN HERRING
'Tis as you said, sir, false and scandalous.

HARMAN Junior
I told you so; all false and scandalous.

ISABINDA
On my soul it is not; her heart speaks in her tongue, and were she silent, her habit and her face speak for her.

BEAMONT
Sir, you have heard the proofs.

FISCAL
Mere allegations, and no proofs. Seem not to believe it, sir.

HARMAN Junior
Well, well, we'll hear it another time.

Captain MIDDLETON
You seem not to believe her testimony, but my whole crew can witness it.

VAN HERRING
Ay, they are all Englishmen.

TOWERSON
That's a nation too generous to do bad actions, and too sincere to justify them done; I wish their neighbours were of the same temper.

HARMAN Junior
Nay, now you kindle, captain; this must not be, we are your friends and servants.

Captain MIDDLETON
'Tis well you are by land, at sea you would be masters: there I myself have met with some affronts, which, though I wanted power then to return, I hailed the captain of the Holland ship, and told him he should dearly answer it, if e'er I met him in the narrow seas. His answer was, (mark but the insolence) If I should hang thee, Middleton, up at thy main yard, and sink thy ship, here's that about my neck—[pointing to his gold chain] would answer it when I came into Holland.

HARMAN Junior
Yes, this is like the other.

TOWERSON
I find we must complain at home; there's no redress to be had here.

ISABINDA
Come, countrywoman,—I must call you so, since he who owns my heart is English born,—be not dejected at your wretched fortune; my house is yours, my clothes shall habit you, even these I wear, rather than see you thus.

HARMAN Junior
Come, come, no more complaints; let us go in; I have ten rummers ready to the bride; as many times shall our guns discharge, to speak the general gladness of this day. I'll lead you, lady.

[Takes the **BRIDE** by the hand.

TOWERSON
A heavy omen to my nuptials!
My countrymen oppressed by sea and land,

And I not able to redress the wrong,
So weak are we, our enemies so strong.

[Exeunt.

ACT IV

SCENE I.—A Wood

Enter **HARMAN Junior**, and **FISCAL**, with swords, and disguised in vizards.

HARMAN Junior
We are disguised enough; the evening now grows dusk.—I would the deed were done!

[Enter **PEREZ** with a **SOLDIER**, and overhears them.

FISCAL
'Twill now be suddenly, if we have courage in this wild woody walk, hot with the feast and plenteous bowls, the bridal company are walking to enjoy the cooling breeze; I spoke to Towerson, as I said I would, and on some private business of great moment, desired that he would leave the company, and meet me single here.

HARMAN Junior
Where if he comes, he never shall return But Towerson stays too long for my revenge; I am in haste to kill him.

FISCAL
He promised me to have been here ere now; if you think fitting, I'll go back and bring him.

HARMAN Junior
Do so, I'll wait you in this place.

[Exit **FISCAL**.

PEREZ
Was ever villany like this of these unknown assassins? Towerson, in vain I saved thy sleeping life if now I let thee lose it, when thou wakest; thou lately hast been bountiful to me, and this way I'll acknowledge it. Yet to disclose their crimes were dangerous. What must I do? This generous Englishman will strait be here, and consultation then perhaps will be too late: I am resolved.—Lieutenant, you have heard, as well as I, the bloody purpose of these men?

SOLDIER
I have, and tremble at the mention of it.

PEREZ
Dare you adventure on an action, as brave as theirs is base?

SOLDIER
Command my life.

PEREZ
No more. Help me despatch that murderer, ere his accomplice comes: the men I know not; but their design is treacherous and bloody.

SOLDIER
And he, they mean to kill, is brave himself, and of a nation I much love.

PEREZ
Come on then.

[Both draw. To **HARMAN Junior**.]

Villain, thou diest, thy conscience tells thee why; I need not urge the crime.

[They assault him.

HARMAN Junior
Murder! I shall be basely murdered; help!

[Enter **TOWERSON**.

TOWERSON
Hold, villains! what unmanly odds is this? Courage, whoe'er thou art; I'll succour thee.

[**TOWERSON** fights with **PEREZ**, and **HARMAN Junior** with the **LIEUTENANT**, and drive them off the stage.

HARMAN Junior
Though, brave unknown, night takes thee from my knowledge, and I want time to thank thee now, take this, and wear it for my sake;

[Gives him a ring.]

Hereafter I'll acknowledge it more largely.

[Exit.

TOWERSON
That voice I've heard; but cannot call to mind, except it be young Harman's. Yet, who should put his life in danger thus? This ring I would not take as salary, but as a gage of his free heart who left it; and, when I know him, I'll restore the pledge. Sure 'twas not far from hence I made the appointment: I know not what this Dutchman's business is, yet, I believe, 'twas somewhat from my rival. It shall go hard, but I will find him out, and then rejoin the company.

[Exit.

[Re-enter **HARMAN Junior**, and **FISCAL**.

FISCAL
The accident was wondrous strange: Did you neither know your assassinates, nor your deliverer?

HARMAN Junior
'Twas all a hurry; yet, upon better recollecting of myself, the man, who freed me, must be Towerson.

FISCAL
Hark, I hear the company walking this way; will you withdraw?

HARMAN Junior
Withdraw, and Isabinda coming!

FISCAL
The wood is full of murderers; every tree, methinks, hides one behind it.

HARMAN Junior
You have two qualities, my friend, that sort but ill together; as mischievous as hell could wish you, but fearful in the execution.

FISCAL
There is a thing within me, called a conscience which is not quite o'ercome; now and then it rebels a little, especially when I am alone, or in the dark.

HARMAN Junior
The moon begins to rise, and glitters through the trees.

ISABINDA [Within.]
Pray let us walk this way; that farther lawn, between the groves, is the most green and pleasant of any in this isle.

HARMAN Junior
I hear my siren's voice, I cannot stir from hence.—Dear friend, if thou wilt e'er oblige me, divert the company a little, and give me opportunity a while to talk alone with her.

FISCAL
You'll get nothing of her, except it be by force.

HARMAN Junior
You know not with what eloquence love may inspire my tongue: The guiltiest wretch, when ready for his sentence, has something still to say.

FISCAL
Well, they come; I'll put you in a way, and wish you good success; but do you hear? remember you are a man, and she a woman; a little force, it may be, would do well.

[Enter **ISABINDA, BEAMONT, MIDDLETON, COLLINS, HARMAN Senior**; and **JULIA**.

ISABINDA
Who saw the bridegroom last?

HARMAN Senior
He refused to pledge the last rummer; so I am out of charity with him.

BEAMONT
Come, shall we backward to the castle? I'll take care of you, lady.

JULIA
Oh, you have drunk so much, you are past all care.

COLLINS
But where can be this jolly bridegroom? Answer me that; I will have the bride satisfied.

FISCAL
He walked alone this way; we met him lately.

ISABINDA
I beseech you, sir, conduct us.

HARMAN Junior
I'll bring you to him, madam.

FISCAL [To **HARMAN Junior**]
Remember, now's your time; if you o'erslip this minute, fortune perhaps will never send another.

HARMAN Junior
I am resolved.

FISCAL
Come, gentlemen, I'll tell you such a pleasant accident, you'll think the evening short.

JULIA
I love a story, and a walk by moonshine.

FISCAL
Lend me your hand then, madam.

[Takes her by the one hand.

BEAMONT
But one, I beseech you then; I must not quit her so.

[Takes her by the other hand. Exeunt.

[Re-enter **HARMAN Junior**, and **ISABINDA**.]

ISABINDA
Come, sir, which is the way? I long to see my love.

HARMAN Junior
You may have your wish, and without stirring hence.

ISABINDA
My love so near? Sure you delight to mock me!

HARMAN Junior
'Tis you delight to torture me; behold the man who loves you more than his own eyes; more than the joys of earth, or hopes of heaven.

ISABINDA
When you renewed your friendship with my Towerson, I thought these vain desires were dead within you.

HARMAN Junior
Smothered they were, not dead; your eyes can kindle no such petty fires, as only blaze a while, and strait go out.

ISABINDA
You know, when I had far less ties upon me, I would not hear you; therefore wonder not if I withdraw, and find the company.

HARMAN Junior
That would be too much cruelty, to make me wretched, and then leave me so.

ISABINDA
Am I in fault if you are miserable? so you may call the rich man's wealth, the cause and object of the robber's guilt. Pray do not persecute me farther: You know I have a husband now, and would be loth to afflict his knowledge with your second folly.

HARMAN Junior
What wondrous care you take to make him happy! yet I approve your method. Ignorance! oh, 'tis a jewel to a husband; that is, 'tis peace in him, 'tis virtue in his wife, 'tis honour in the world; he has all this, while he is ignorant.

ISABINDA
You pervert my meaning: I would not keep my actions from his knowledge; your bold attempts I would: But yet henceforth conceal your impious flames; I shall not ever be thus indulgent to your shame, to keep it from his notice.

HARMAN Junior

You are a woman; have enough of love for him and me; I know the plenteous harvest all is his: He has so much of joy, that he must labour under it. In charity, you may allow some gleanings to a friend.

ISABINDA
Now you grow rude: I'll hear no more.

HARMAN Junior
You must.

ISABINDA
Leave me.

HARMAN Junior
I cannot.

ISABINDA
I find I must be troubled with this idle talk some minutes more, but 'tis your last.

HARMAN Junior
And therefore I'll improve it: Pray, resolve to make me happy by your free consent. I do not love these half enjoyments, to enervate my delights with using force, and neither give myself nor you that full content, which two can never have, but where both join with equal eagerness to bless each other.

ISABINDA
Bless me, ye kind inhabitants of heaven, from hearing words like these!

HARMAN Junior
You must do more than hear them. You know you were now going to your bridal-bed. Call your own thoughts but to a strict account, they'll tell you, all this day your fancy ran on nothing else; 'tis but the same scene still you were to act; only the person changed,—it may be for the better.

ISABINDA
You dare not, sure, attempt this villany.

HARMAN Junior
Call not the act of love by that gross name; you'll give it a much better when 'tis done, and woo me to a second.

ISABINDA
Dost thou not fear a heaven?

HARMAN Junior
No, I hope one in you. Do it, and do it heartily; time is precious; it will prepare you better for your husband. Come—

[Lays hold on her.

ISABINDA

O mercy, mercy! Oh, pity your own soul, and pity mine; think how you'll wish undone this horrid act, when your hot lust is slaked; think what will follow when my husband knows it, if shame will let me live to tell it him; and tremble at a Power above, who sees, and surely will revenge it.

HARMAN Junior
I have thought!

ISABINDA
Then I am sure you're penitent.

HARMAN Junior
No, I only gave you scope, to let you see, all you have urged I knew: You find 'tis to no purpose either to talk or strive.

ISABINDA [Running.]

Some succour! help, oh help!

[She breaks from him.

HARMAN Junior [Running after her.]
That too is vain, you cannot 'scape me.

[Exit.

HARMAN Junior [Within.]
Now you are mine; yield, or by force I'll take it.

ISABINDA [Within.]
Oh, kill me first!

HARMAN Junior [Within.]
I'll bear you where your cries shall not be heard.

ISABINDA [As further off.]
Succour, sweet heaven! oh succour me!

SCENE II

Enter **HARMAN Senior, FISCAL, VAN HERRING, BEAMONT, COLLINS,** and **JULIA.**

BEAMONT
You have led us here a fairy's round in the moonshine, to seek a bridegroom in a wood, till we have lost the bride.

COLLINS

I wonder what's become of her?

HARMAN Senior
Got together, got together, I warrant you, before this time; you Englishmen are so hot, you cannot stay for ceremonies. A good honest Dutchman would have been plying the glass all this while, and drunk to the hopes of Hans in Kelder till 'twas bed-time.

BEAMONT
Yes, and then have rolled into the sheets, and turned o' the t'other side to snore, without so much as a parting blow; till about midnight he would have wakened in a maze, and found first he was married by putting forth a foot, and feeling a woman by him; and, it may be, then, instead of kissing, desired yough Fro to hold his head.

COLLINS
And by that night's work have given her a proof, what she might expect for ever after.

BEAMONT
In my conscience, you Hollanders never get your children, but in the spirit of brandy; you are exalted then a little above your natural phlegm, and only that, which can make you fight, and destroy men, makes you get them.

FISCAL
You may live to know, that we can kill men when we are sober.

BEAMONT
Then they must be drunk, and not able to defend themselves.

JULIA
Pray leave this talk, and let us try if we can surprise the lovers under some convenient tree: Shall we separate, and look them?

BEAMONT
Let you and I go together then, and if we cannot find them, we shall do as good, for we shall find one another.

FISCAL
Pray take that path, or that; I will pursue this.

[Exeunt all but the **FISCAL**.

FISCAL
So, now I have diverted them from Harman, I'll look for him myself, and see how he speeds in his adventure.

[Enter **HARMAN Junior**.

HARMAN Junior
Who goes there?

FISCAL
A friend: I was just in quest of you, so are all the company: Where have you left the bride?

HARMAN Junior
Tied to a tree and gagged, and—

FISCAL
And what? Why do you stare and tremble? Answer me like a man.

HARMAN Junior
Oh, I have nothing left of manhood in me! I am turned beast or devil. Have I not horns, and tail, and leathern wings? Methinks I should have by my actions. Oh, I have done a deed so ill, I cannot name it.

FISCAL
Not name it, and yet do it? That's a fool's modesty: Come, I'll name it for you: You have enjoyed your mistress.

HARMAN Junior
How easily so great a villany comes from thy mouth! I have done worse, I have ravished her.

FISCAL
That's no harm, so you have killed her afterwards.

HARMAN Junior
Killed her! why thou art a worse fiend than I.

FISCAL
Those fits of conscience in another might be excusable; but in you, a Dutchman, who are of a race that are born rebels, and live every where on rapine,—would you degenerate, and have remorse? Pray, what makes any thing a sin but law? and, what law is there here against it? Is not your father chief? Will he condemn you for a petty rape? the woman an Amboyner, and, what's less, now married to an Englishman! Come, if there be a hell, 'tis but for those that sin in Europe, not for us in Asia; heathens have no hell. Tell me, how was't? Pr'ythee, the history.

HARMAN Junior
I forced her. What resistance she could make she did, but 'twas in vain; I bound her, as I told you, to a tree.

FISCAL
And she exclaimed, I warrant—

HARMAN Junior
Yes; and called heaven and earth to witness.

FISCAL
Not after it was done?

HARMAN Junior
More than before—desired me to have killed her. Even when I had not left her power to speak, she curst me with her eyes.

FISCAL
Nay, then, you did not please her; if you had, she ne'er had cursed you heartily. But we lose time: Since you have done this action, 'tis necessary you proceed; we must have no tales told.

HARMAN Junior
What do you mean?

FISCAL
To dispatch her immediately; could you be so senseless to ravish her, and let her live? What if her husband should have found her? What if any other English? Come, there's no dallying; it must be done: My other plot is ripe, which shall destroy them all to-morrow.

HARMAN Junior
I love her still to madness, and never can consent to have her killed. We'll thence remove her, if you please, and keep her safe till your intended plot shall take effect; and when her husband's gone, I'll win her love by every circumstance of kindness.

FISCAL
You may do so; but t'other is the safer way: But I'll not stand with you for one life. I could have wished that Towerson had been killed before I had proceeded to my plot; but since it cannot be, we must go on; conduct me where you left her.

HARMAN Junior
Oh, that I could forget both act and place!

[Exeunt.

SCENE III

SCENE drawn, discovers **ISABINDA** bound.

Enter **TOWERSON**.

TOWERSON
Sure I mistook the place; I'll wait no longer:
Something within me does forebode me ill;
I stumbled when I entered first this wood;
My nostrils bled three drops; then stopped the blood,
And not one more would follow.—
What's that, which seems to bear a mortal shape,

[Sees **ISABINDA**

Yet neither stirs nor speaks? or, is it some
Illusion of the night? some spectre, such
As in these Asian parts more frequently appear?
Whate'er it be, I'll venture to approach it.

[Goes near.

My Isabinda bound and gagged! Ye powers,
I tremble while I free her, and scarce dare
Restore her liberty of speech, for fear
Of knowing more.

[Unbinds her, and ungags her.

ISABINDA
No longer bridegroom thou, nor I a bride;
Those names are vanished; love is now no more;
Look on me as thou would'st on some foul leper;
And do not touch me; I am all polluted,
All shame, all o'er dishonour; fly my sight,
And, for my sake, fly this detested isle,
Where horrid ills so black and fatal dwell,
As Indians could not guess, till Europe taught.

TOWERSON
Speak plainer, I am recollected now:
I know I am a man, the sport of fate;
Yet, oh my better half, had heaven so pleased,
I had been more content, to suffer in myself than thee!

ISABINDA
What shall I say! That monster of a man,
Harman,—now I have named him, think the rest,—
Alone, and singled like a timorous hind
From the full herd, by flattery drew me first,
Then forced me to an act, so base and brutal!
Heaven knows my innocence: But, why do I
Call that to witness!
Heaven saw, stood silent: Not one flash of lightning
Shot from the conscious firmament, to shew its justice:
Oh had it struck us both, it had saved me!

TOWERSON
Heaven suffered more in that, than you, or I,
Wherefore have I been faithful to my trust,
True to my love, and tender to the opprest?

Am I condemned to be the second man,
Who e'er complained he virtue served in vain?
But dry your tears, these sufferings all are mine.
Your breast is white, and cold as falling snow;
You, still as fragrant as your eastern groves;
And your whole frame as innocent, and holy,
As if your being were all soul and spirit,
Without the gross allay of flesh and blood.
Come to my arms again!

ISABINDA
O never, never!
I am not worthy now; my soul indeed
Is free from sin; but the foul speckled stains
Are from my body ne'er to be washed out,
But in my death. Kill me, my love, or I
Must kill myself; else you may think I was
A black adultress in my mind, and some
Of me consented.

TOWERSON
Your wish to die, shews you deserve to live.
I have proclaimed you guiltless to myself.
Self-homicide, which was, in heathens, honour,
In us, is only sin.

ISABINDA
I thought the Eternal Mind
Had made us masters of these mortal frames;
You told me, he had given us wills to chuse,
And reason to direct us in our choice;
If so, why should he tie us up from dying,
When death's the greater good?

TOWERSON
Can death, which is our greatest enemy, be good?
Death is the dissolution of our nature;
And nature therefore does abhor it most,
Whose greatest law is—to preserve our beings.

ISABINDA
I grant, it is its great and general law:
But as kings, who are, or should be, above laws,
Dispense with them when levelled at themselves;
Even so may man, without offence to heaven,
Dispense with what concerns himself alone.
Nor is death in itself an ill;
Then holy martyrs sinned, who ran uncalled

To snatch their martyrdom; and blessed virgins,
Whom you celebrate for voluntary death,
To free themselves from that which I have suffered.

TOWERSON
They did it, to prevent what might ensue;
Your shame's already past.

ISABINDA
It may return,
If I am yet so mean to live a little longer.

TOWERSON
You know not; heaven may give you succour yet;
You see it sends me to you.

ISABINDA
'Tis too late,
You should have come before.

TOWERSON
You may live to see yourself revenged.
Come, you shall stay for that, then I'll die with you,
You have convinced my reason, nor am I
Ashamed to learn from you.
To heaven's tribunal my appeal I make;
If as a governor he sets me here,
To guard this weak-built citadel of life,
When 'tis no longer to be held, I may
With honour quit the fort. But first I'll both
Revenge myself and you.

ISABINDA
Alas! you cannot take revenge; your countrymen
Are few, and those unarmed.

TOWERSON
Though not on all the nation, as I would,
Yet I at least can take it on the man.

ISABINDA
Leave me to heaven's revenge, for thither I
Will go, and plead, myself, my own just cause.
There's not an injured saint of all my sex,
But kindly will conduct me to my judge,
And help me tell my story.

TOWERSON

I'll send the offender first, though to that place
He never can arrive: Ten thousand devils,
Damned for less crimes than he,
And Tarquin in their head, way-lay his soul,
To pull him down in triumph, and to shew him
In pomp among his countrymen; for sure
Hell has its Netherlands, and its lowest country
Must be their lot.

[Enter **HARMAN Junior**, and **FISCAL**.

HARMAN Junior
'Twas hereabout I left her tied. The rage of love renews again within me.

FISCAL
She'll like the effects on't better now. By this time it has sunk into her imagination, and given her a more pleasing idea of the man, who offered her so sweet a violence.

ISABINDA
Save me, sweet heaven! the monster comes again!

HARMAN Junior
Oh, here she is.—My own fair bride,—for so you are, not Towerson's,—let me unbind you; I expect that you should bind yourself about me now, and tie me in your arms.

TOWERSON [Drawing.]
No, villain, no! hot satyr of the woods,
Expect another entertainment now.
Behold revenge for injured chastity.
This sword heaven draws against thee,
And here has placed me like a fiery cherub,
To guard this paradise from any second violation.

FISCAL
We must dispatch him, sir, we have the odds;
And when he's killed, leave me t'invent the excuse.

HARMAN Junior
Hold a little: As you shunned fighting formerly with me, so would I now with you. The mischiefs I have done are past recal. Yield then your useless right in her I love, since the possession is no longer yours; so is your honour safe, and so is hers, the husband only altered.

TOWERSON
You trifle; there's no room for treaty here:
The shame's too open, and the wrong too great.
Now all the saints in heaven look down to see
The justice I shall do, for 'tis their cause;
And all the fiends below prepare thy tortures.

ISABINDA
If Towerson would, think'st thou my soul so poor,
To own thy sin, and make the base act mine,
By chusing him who did it? Know, bad man,
I'll die with him, but never live with thee.

TOWERSON
Prepare; I shall suspect you stay for further help,
And think not this enough.

FISCAL
We are ready for you.

HARMAN Junior
Stand back! I'll fight with him alone.

FISCAL
Thank you for that; so, if he kills you, I shall have him single upon me.

[All three fight.

ISABINDA
Heaven assist my love!

HARMAN Junior
There, Englishman, 'twas meant well to thy heart.

[**TOWERSON** wounded.

FISCAL
Oh you can bleed, I see, for all your cause.

TOWERSON
Wounds but awaken English courage.

HARMAN Junior
Yet yield me Isabinda, and be safe.

TOWERSON
I'll fight myself all scarlet over first;
Were there no love, or no revenge,
I could not now desist, in point of honour.

HARMAN Junior
Resolve me first one question:
Did you not draw your sword this night before,
To rescue one opprest with odds?

TOWERSON
Yes, in this very wood: I bear a ring,
The badge of gratitude from him I saved.

HARMAN Junior
This ring was mine; I should be loth to kill
The frank redeemer of my life.

TOWERSON
I quit that obligation. But we lose time.
Come, ravisher!

[They fight again, **TOWERSON** closes with **HARMAN Junior** and gets him down; as he is going to kill him, the **FISCAL** gets over him.

FISCAL
Hold, and let him rise; for if you kill him,
At the same instant you die too.

TOWERSON
Dog, do thy worst, for I would so be killed;
I'll carry his soul captive with me into the other world.

[Stabs **HARMAN Junior**.

HARMAN Junior
O mercy, mercy, heaven!

[Dies.

FISCAL
Take this, then; in return.

[As he is going to stab him, **ISABINDA** takes hold of his hand.

ISABINDA
Hold, hold; the weak may give some help.

TOWERSON [Rising.]
Now, sir, I am for you.

FISCAL [Retiring.]
Hold, sir, there is no more resistance made.
I beg you, by the honour of your nation,
Do not pursue my life; I tender you my sword.

[Holds his sword by the point to him.

TOWERSON
Base beyond example of any country, but thy own!

ISABINDA
Kill him, sweet love, or we shall both repent it.

FISCAL [Kneeling to her.]
Divinest beauty! Abstract of all that's
excellent in woman, can you be friend to murder?

ISABINDA
'Tis none to kill a villain, and a Dutchman.

FISCAL [Kneeling to **TOWERSON**.]
Noble Englishman, give me my life, unworthy of your taking! By all that is good and holy here I swear,
before the governor to plead your cause; and to declare his son's detested crime, so to secure your lives.

TOWERSON
Rise, take thy life, though I can scarce believe thee;
If for a coward it be possible, become an honest man.

[Enter **HARMAN Senior, VAN HERRING, BEAMONT, COLLINS, JULIA,** the **GOVERNORS GUARD**.]

FISCAL [To **HARMAN Senior**]
Oh, sir, you come in time to rescue me;
The greatest villain, who this day draws breath,
Stands here before your eyes: behold your son,
That worthy, sweet, unfortunate young man,
Lies there, the last cold breath yet hovering
Betwixt his trembling lips.

TOWERSON
Oh, monster of ingratitude!

HARMAN Senior
Oh, my unfortunate old age, whose prop
And only staff is gone, dead ere I die!
These should have been his tears, and I have been
That body to be mourned.

BEAMONT
I am so much amazed, I scarce believe my senses.

FISCAL
And will you let him live, who did this act?
Shall murder, and of your own son,
And such a son, go free; He lives too long,

By this one minute which he stays behind him.

ISABINDA
Oh, sir, remember, in that place you hold,
You are a common father to us all;
We beg but justice of you; hearken first
To my lamented story.

FISCAL
First hear me, sir.

TOWERSON
Thee, slave! thou livest but by the breath I gave thee.
Didst thou but now plead on thy knees for life,
And offer'dst to make known my innocence
In Harman's injuries?

FISCAL
I offered to have cleared thy innocence,
Who basely murdered him!—But words are needless;
Sir, you see evidence before your eyes,
And I the witness, on my oath to heaven,
How clear your son, how criminal this man.

COLLINS
Towerson could do nothing but what was noble.

BEAMONT
We know his native worth.

FISCAL
His worth! Behold it on the murderer's hand;
A robber first, he took degrees in mischief,
And grew to what he is: Know you that diamond,
And whose it was? See if he dares deny it.

TOWERSON
Sir, it was your son's, that freely I acknowledge;
But how I came by it—

HARMAN Senior
No, it is too much, I'll hear no more.

FISCAL
The devil of jealousy, and that of avarice, both, I believe, possest him; or your son was innocently talking with his wife, and he perhaps had found them; this I guess, but saw it not, because I came too late. I only viewed the sweet youth just expiring, and Towerson stooping down to take the ring; she kneeling by to

help him: when he saw me, he would, you may be sure, have sent me after, because I was a witness of the fact. This on my soul is true.

TOWERSON
False as that soul, each word, each syllable;
The ring he put upon my hand this night,
When in this wood unknown, and near this place,
Without my timely help he had been slain.

FISCAL
See this unlikely story!
What enemies had he, who should assault him?
Or is it probable that very man,
Who actually did kill him afterwards,
Should save his life so little time before?

ISABINDA
Base man, thou knowest the reason of his death;
He had committed on my person, sir,
An impious rape; first tied me to that tree,
And there my husband found me, whose revenge
Was such, as heaven and earth will justify.

HARMAN Senior
I know not what heaven will, but earth shall not.

BEAMONT
Her story carries such a face of truth,
Ye cannot but believe it.

COLLINS
The other, a malicious ill-patched lie.

FISCAL
Yes, you are proper judges of his crime,
Who, with the rest of your accomplices,
Your countrymen, and Towerson the chief,
Whom we too kindly used, would have surprised
The fort, and made us slaves; that shall be proved,
More soon than you imagine; I found it out
This evening.

TOWERSON
Sure the devil has lent thee all his stock of falsehood, and must be forced hereafter to tell truth.

BEAMONT
Sir, it is impossible you should believe it.

HARMAN Senior
Seize them all.

COLLINS
You cannot be so base.

HARMAN Senior
I'll be so just, 'till I can hear your plea
Against this plot; which if not proved, and fully,
You are quit; mean time, resistance is but vain.

TOWERSON
Provided that we may have equal hearing,
I am content to yield, though I declare,
You have no power to judge us.

[Gives his sword.

BEAMONT
Barbarous, ungrateful Dutch!

HARMAN Senior
See them conveyed apart to several prisons,
Lest they combine to forge some specious lie
In their excuse.
Let Towerson and that woman too be parted.

ISABINDA
Was ever such a sad divorce made on a bridal night!
But we before were parted, ne'er to meet.
Farewell, farewell, my last and only love!

TOWERSON
Curse on my fond credulity, to think
There could be faith or honour in the Dutch!—
Farewell my Isabinda, and farewell,
My much wronged countrymen! remember yet,
That no unmanly weakness in your sufferings
Disgrace the native honour of our isle:
For you I mourn, grief for myself were vain;
I have lost all, and now would lose my pain.

[Exeunt.

ACT V

SCENE I.—A Table Set Out

Enter **HARMAN Senior**, **FISCAL**, **VAN HERRING**, and two **DUTCHMEN**: They sit. **BOY**, and **WAITERS**, **GUARDS**.

HARMAN Senior
My sorrow cannot be so soon digested for losing of a son I loved so well; but I consider great advantages must with some loss be bought; as this rich trade which I this day have purchased with his death: yet let me lie revenged, and I shall still live on, and eat and drink down all my griefs. Now to the matter, Fiscal.

FISCAL
Since we may freely speak among ourselves, all I have said of Towerson was most false. You were consenting, sir, as well as I, that Perez should be hired to murder him, which he refusing when he was engaged, 'tis dangerous to let him longer live.

VAN HERRING
Dispatch him; he will be a shrewd witness against us, if he returns to Europe.

FISCAL
I have thought better, if you please,—to kill him by form of law, as accessary to the English plot, which I have long been forging.

HARMAN Senior
Send one to seize him strait.

[Exit a **MESSENGER**.]

But what you said, that Towerson was guiltless of my son's death, I easily believe, and never thought otherwise, though I dissembled.

VAN HERRING
Nor I; but it was well done to feign that story.

1ST DUTCHMAN
The true one was too foul.

2ND DUTCHMAN
And afterwards to draw the English off from his concernment, to their own, I think 'twas rarely managed that.

HARMAN Senior
So far, 'twas well; now to proceed, for I would gladly know, whether the grounds are plausible enough of this pretended plot.

FISCAL
With favour of this honourable court, give me but leave to smooth the way before you. Some two or three nights since, (it matters not,) a Japan soldier, under captain Perez, came to a centinel upon the guard, and in familiar talk did question him about this castle, of its strength, and how he thought it

might be taken; this discourse the other told me early the next morning: I thereupon did issue private orders, to rack the Japanese, myself being present.

HARMAN Senior
But what's this to the English?

FISCAL
You shall hear: I asked him, when his pains were strongest on him, if Towerson, or the English factory, had never hired him to betray the fort? he answered, (as it was true) they never had; nor was his meaning more in that discourse, than as a soldier to inform himself, and so to pass the time.

VAN HERRING
Did he confess no more?

FISCAL
You interrupt me. I told him, I was certainly informed the English had designs upon the castle, and if he frankly would confess their plot, he should not only be released from torment, but bounteously rewarded: Present pain and future hope, in fine, so wrought upon him, he yielded to subscribe whatever I pleased; and so he stands committed.

HARMAN Senior
Well contrived; a fair way made, upon this accusation, to put them all to torture.

2ND DUTCHMAN
By his confession, all of them shall die, even to their general, Towerson.

HARMAN Senior
He stands convicted of another crime, for which he is to suffer.

FISCAL
This does well to help it though: For Towerson is here a person publicly employed from England, and if he should appeal, as sure he will, you have no power to judge him in Amboyna.

VAN HERRING
But in regard of the late league and union betwixt the nations, how can this be answered?

1ST DUTCHMAN
To torture subjects to so great a king, a pain never heard of in their happy land, will sound but ill in Europe.

FISCAL
Their English laws in England have their force; and we have ours, different from theirs at home. It is enough, they either shall confess, or we will falsify their hands to make them. Then, for the apology, let me alone; I have it writ already to a title, of what they shall subscribe; this I will publish, and make our most unheard of cruelties to seem most just and legal.

HARMAN Senior

Then, in the name of him, who put it first into thy head to form this damned false plot, proceed we to the execution of it. And to begin; first seize we their effects, rifle their chests, their boxes, writings, books, and take of them a seeming inventory; but all to our own use.—I shall grow young with thought of this, and lose my son's remembrance!

FISCAL
Will you not please to call the prisoners in? At least inquire what torments have extorted.

HARMAN Senior
Go thou and bring us word.

[Exit **FISCAL**.]

Boy, give me some tobacco, and a stoup of wine, boy.

BOY
I shall, sir.

HARMAN Senior
And a tub to leak in, boy; when was this table without a leaking vessel?

VAN HERRING
That's an omission.

1ST DUTCHMAN
A great omission. 'Tis a member of the table, I take it so.

HARMAN Senior
Never any thing of moment was done at our council-table without a leaking tub, at least in my time; great affairs require great consultations, great consultations require great drinking, and great drinking a great leaking vessel.

VAN HERRING
I am even drunk with joy already, to see our godly business in this forwardness.

[Enter **FISCAL**.

HARMAN Senior
Where are the prisoners?

FISCAL
At the door.

HARMAN Senior
Bring them in; I'll try if we can face them down by impudence, and make them to confess.

[Enter **BEAMONT** and **COLLINS**, guarded.

You are not ignorant of our business with you: the cries of your accomplices have already reached your ears; and your own consciences, above a thousand summons, a thousand tortures, instruct you what to do. No farther juggling, nothing but plain sincerity and truth to be delivered now; a free confession will first atone for all your sins above, and may do much below to gain your pardons. Let me exhort you, therefore, be you merciful, first to yourselves and make acknowledgment of your conspiracy.

BEAMONT
What conspiracy?

FISCAL
Why la you, that the devil should go masked with such a seeming honest face! I warrant you know of no such thing.

HARMAN Senior
Were not you, Mr Beamont, and you, Collins both accessary to the horrid plot, for the surprisal of this fort and island?

BEAMONT
As I shall reconcile my sins to heaven, in my last article of life, I am innocent.

COLLINS
And so am I.

HARMAN Senior
So, you are first upon the negative.

BEAMONT
And will be so till death.

COLLINS
What plot is this you speak of?

FISCAL
Here are impudent rogues! now after confession of two Japanese, these English starts dare ask what plot it is!

HARMAN Senior
Not to inform your knowledge, but that law may have its course in every circumstance, Fiscal, sum up their accusation to them.

FISCAL
You stand accused, that new-year's day last past, there met at captain Towerson's house, you present, and many others of your factory: There, against law and justice, and all ties of friendship, and of partnership betwixt us, you did conspire to seize upon the fort, to murder this our worthy governor; and, by the help of your plantations near, of Jacatra, Banda, and Loho, to keep it for yourselves.

BEAMONT
What proofs have you of this?

FISCAL
The confession of two Japanese, hired by you to attempt it.

BEAMONT
I hear they have been forced by torture to it.

HARMAN Senior
It matters not which way the truth comes out; take heed, for their example is before you.

BEAMONT
Ye have no right, ye dare not torture us; we owe you no subjection.

FISCAL
That, sir, must be disputed at the Hague; in the mean time we are in possession here.

2ND DUTCHMAN
And we can make ourselves to be obeyed.

VAN HERRING
In few words, gentlemen, confess. There is a beverage ready for you else, which you will not like to swallow.

COLLINS
How is this?

HARMAN Senior
You shall be muffled up like ladies, with an oiled cloth put underneath your chins, then water poured above; which either you must drink, or must not breathe.

1ST DUTCHMAN
That is one way, we have others.

HARMAN Senior
Yes, we have two elements at your service, fire, as well as water; certain things called matches to be tied to your finger-ends, which are as sovereign as nutmegs to quicken your short memories.

BEAMONT
You are inhuman, to make your cruelty your pastime: nature made me a man, and not a whale, to swallow down a flood.

HARMAN Senior
You will grow a corpulent gentleman like me; I shall love you the better for it; now you are but a spare rib.

FISCAL
These things are only offered to your choice; you may avoid your tortures, and confess.

COLLINS
Kill us first; for that we know is your design at last, and 'tis more mercy now.

BEAMONT
Be kind, and execute us while we bear the shapes of men, ere fire and water have destroyed our figures; let me go whole out of the world, I care not, and find my body when I rise again, so as I need not be ashamed of it.

HARMAN Senior
'Tis well you are merry; will you yet confess?

BEAMONT
Never.

HARMAN Senior
Bear them away to torture.

VAN HERRING
We will try your constancy.

BEAMONT
We will shame your cruelty; if we deserve our tortures, 'tis first for freeing such an infamous nation, that ought to have been slaves, and then for trusting them as partners, who had cast off the yoke of their lawful sovereign.

HARMAN Senior
Away, I'll hear no more.—Now who comes the next?

[Exeunt the **ENGLISH** with a **GUARD**.

FISCAL
Towerson's page, a ship-boy, and a woman.

HARMAN Senior
Call them in.

[Exit a **MESSENGER**.

VAN HERRING
We shall have easy work with them.

FISCAL
Not so easy as you imagine, they have endured the beverage already; all masters of their pain, no one confessing.

HARMAN Senior
The devil's in these English! those brave boys would prove stout topers if they lived.

[Enter **PAGE**, a **BOY**, and a **WOMAN**, led as from torture.

Come hither, ye perverse imps; they say you have endured the water torment, we will try what fire will do with you: You, sirrah, confess; were not you knowing of Towerson's plot, against this fort and island?

PAGE
I have told your hangman no, twelve times within this hour, when I was at the last gasp; and that is a time, I think, when a man should not dissemble.

HARMAN Senior
A man! mark you that now; you English boys have learnt a trick of late, of growing men betimes; and doing men's work, too, before you come to twenty.

VAN HERRING
Sirrah, I will try if you are a salamander and can live in the fire.

PAGE
Sure you think my father got me of some Dutchwoman, and that I am but a half-strain courage; but you shall find that I am all over English as well in fire as water.

BOY
Well, of all religions, I do not like your Dutch.

FISCAL
No? and why, young stripling?

BOY
Because your penance comes before confession.

HARMAN Senior
Do you mock us, sirrah? To the fire with him.

BOY
Do so; all you shall get by it is this; before I answered no; now I'll be sullen and will talk no more.

HARMAN Senior
Best cutting off these little rogues betime; if they grow men, they will have the spirit of revenge in them.

PAGE
Yes, as your children have that of rebellion. Oh that I could but live to be governor here, to make your fat guts pledge me in that beverage I drunk, you Sir John Falstaff of Amsterdam!

BOY
I have a little brother in England, that I intend to appear to when you have killed me; and if he does not promise me the death of ten Dutchmen in the next war, I'll haunt him instead of you.

HARMAN Senior
What say you, woman? Have compassion of yourself, and confess; you are of a softer sex.

WOMAN
But of a courage full as manly; there is no sex in souls; would you have English wives shew less of bravery than their children do? To lie by an Englishman's side, is enough to give a woman resolution.

FISCAL
Here is a hen of the game too, but we shall tame you in the fire.

WOMAN
My innocence shall there be tried like gold, till it come out the purer. When you have burnt me all into one wound, cram gunpowder into it, and blow me up, I'll not confess one word to shame my country.

HARMAN Senior
I think we have got here the mother of the Maccabees; away with them all three.

[Exeunt the **ENGLISH** guarded.]

I'll take the pains myself to see these tortured.

[Exeunt **HARMAN, VAN HERRING**, and the two **DUTCHMEN** with the **ENGLISH**: Manet **FISCAL**.

[Enter **JULIA** to the **FISCAL**.

JULIA
Oh you have ruined me! you have undone me, in the person of my husband!

FISCAL
If he will needs forfeit his life to the laws, by joining with the English in a plot, it is not in me to save him; but, dearest Julia, be satisfied, you shall not want a husband.

JULIA
Do you think I'll ever come into a bed with him, who robbed me of my dear sweet man?

FISCAL
Dry up your tears; I am in earnest; I will marry you; i'faith I will; it is your destiny.

JULIA
Nay if it be my destiny—but I vow I'll never be yours but upon one condition.

FISCAL
Name your desire, and take it.

JULIA
Then save poor Beamont's life.

FISCAL
This is the most unkind request you could have made; it shews you love him better: therefore, in prudence, I should haste his death.

JULIA
Come, I'll not be denied; you shall give me his life, or I'll not love you; by this kiss you shall, child.

FISCAL
Pray ask some other thing.

JULIA
I have your word for this, and if you break it, how shall I trust you for your marrying me?

FISCAL [Aside.
Well, I will do it to oblige you. But to prevent her new designs with him, I'll see him shipped away for England strait.

JULIA
I may build upon your promise, then?

FISCAL
Most firmly: I hear company.

[Enter **HARMAN Senior, VAN HERRING**, and the two **DUTCHMEN**, with **TOWERSON** prisoner.

HARMAN Senior
Now, captain Towerson, you have had the privilege to be examined last; this on the score of my old friendship with you, though you have ill deserved it. But here you stand accused of no less crimes than robbery first, then murder, and last, treason: What can you say to clear yourself?

TOWERSON
You're interested in all, and therefore partial:
I have considered on it, and will not plead,
Because I know you have no right to judge me;
For the last treaty betwixt our king and you
Expressly said, that causes criminal
Were first to be examined, and then judged,
Not here, but by the Council of Defence;
To whom I make appeal.

FISCAL
This court conceives that it has power to judge you, derived from the most high and mighty states, who in this island are supreme, and that as well in criminal as civil causes.

1ST DUTCHMAN
You are not to question the authority of the court, which is to judge you.

TOWERSON
Sir, by your favour, I both must, and will:
I'll not so far betray my nation's right;
We are not here your subjects, but your partners:

And that supremacy of power, you claim,
Extends but to the natives, not to us:
Dare you, who in the British seas strike sail,
Nay more, whose lives and freedom are our alms,
Presume to sit and judge your benefactors?
Your base new upstart commonwealth should blush,
To doom the subjects of an English king,
The meanest of whose merchants would disdain
The narrow life, and the domestic baseness,
Of one of those you call your Mighty States.

FISCAL
You spend your breath in railing; speak to the purpose.

HARMAN Senior
Hold yet: Because you shall not call us cruel,
Or plead I would be judge in my own cause,
I shall accept of that appeal you make,
Concerning my son's death; provided first,
You clear yourself from what concerns the public;
For that relating to our general safety,
The judgment of it cannot be deferred,
But with our common danger.

TOWERSON
Let me first
Be bold to question you: What circumstance
Can make this, your pretended plot, seem likely?
The natives, first, you tortured; their confession,
Extorted so, can prove no crime in us.
Consider, next, the strength of this your castle;
Its garrison above two hundred men,
Besides as many of your city burghers,
All ready on the least alarm, or summons,
To reinforce the others; for ten English,
And merchants they, not soldiers, with the aid
Of ten Japanners, all of them unarmed,
Except five swords, and not so many muskets,—
The attempt had only been for fools or madmen.

FISCAL
We cannot help your want of wit; proceed.

TOWERSON
Grant then we had been desperate enough
To hazard this; we must at least forecast,
How to secure possession when we had it.
We had no ship nor pinnace in the harbour,

Nor could have aid from any factory:
The nearest to us forty leagues from hence,
And they but few in number: You, besides
This fort, have yet three castles in this isle,
Amply provided for, and eight tall ships
Riding at anchor near; consider this,
And think what all the world will judge of it.

HARMAN Senior
Nothing but falsehood is to be expected
From such a tongue, whose heart is fouled with treason.
Give him the beverage.

FISCAL
'Tis ready, sir.

HARMAN Senior
Hold; I have some reluctance to proceed
To that extremity: He was my friend,
And I would have him frankly to confess:
Push open that prison door, and set before him
The image of his pains in other men.

[The SCENE opens, and discovers the **ENGLISH** tortured, and the **DUTCH** tormenting them.

FISCAL
Now, sir, how does the object like you?

TOWERSON
Are you men or devils! D'Alva, whom you
Condemn for cruelty, did ne'er the like;
He knew original villany was in your blood.
Your fathers all are damned for their rebellion;
When they rebelled, they were well used to this.
These tortures ne'er were hatched in human breasts;
But as your country lies confined on hell,
Just on its marches, your black neighbours taught ye;
And just such pains as you invent on earth,
Hell has reserved for you.

HARMAN Senior
Are you yet moved?

TOWERSON
But not as you would have me.
I could weep tears of blood to view this usage;
But you, as if not made of the same mould,
See, with dry eyes, the miseries of men,

As they were creatures of another kind,
Not Christians, nor allies, nor partners with you,
But as if beasts, transfixed on theatres,
To make you cruel sport.

HARMAN Senior
These are but vulgar objects; bring his friend,
Let him behold his tortures; shut that door.

[The Scene closed.

[Enter **BEAMONT**, led with matches tied to his hands.

TOWERSON [Embracing him.]
Oh my dear friend, now I am truly wretched!
Even in that part which is most sensible,
My friendship:
How have we lived to see the English name
The scorn of these, the vilest of mankind!

BEAMONT
Courage, my friend, and rather praise we heaven,
That it has chose two, such as you and me,
Who will not shame our country with our pains,
But stand, like marble statues, in their fires,
Scorched and defaced, perhaps, not melted down.
So let them burn this tenement of earth;
They can but burn me naked to my soul;
That's of a nobler frame, and will stand firm,
Upright, and unconsumed.

FISCAL
Confess; if you have kindness, save your friend.

TOWERSON
Yes, by my death I would, not my confession:
He is so brave, he would not so be saved;
But would renounce a friendship built on shame.

HARMAN Senior
Bring more candles, and burn him from the wrists up to the elbows.

BEAMONT
Do; I'll enjoy the flames like Scævola;
And, when one's roasted, give the other hand.

TOWERSON
Let me embrace you while you are a man.

Now you must lose that form; be parched and rivelled,
Like a dried mummy, or dead malefactor,
Exposed in chains, and blown about by winds.

BEAMONT
Yet this I can endure.
Go on, and weary out two elements;
Vex fire and water with the experiments
Of pains far worse than death.

TOWERSON
Oh, let me take my turn!
You will have double pleasure; I'm ashamed
To be the only Englishman untortured.

VAN HERRING
You soon should have your wish, but that we know In him you suffer more.

HARMAN Senior
Fill me a brim-full glass:
Now, captain, here's to all your countrymen;
I wish your whole East India company
Were in this room, that we might use them thus.

FISCAL
They should have fires of cloves and cinnamon;
We would cut down whole groves to honour them,
And be at cost to burn them nobly.

BEAMONT
Barbarous villains! now you show yourselves

HARMAN Senior
Boy, take that candle thence, and bring it hither;
I am exalted, and would light my pipe
Just where the wick is fed with English fat.

VAN HERRING
So would I; oh, the tobacco tastes divinely after it.

TOWERSON
We have friends in England, who would weep to see
This acted on a theatre, which here
You make your pastime.

BEAMONT
Oh, that this flesh were turned a cake of ice,
That I might in an instant melt away,

And become nothing, to escape this torment!
There is not cold enough in all the north
To quench my burning blood.

[**FISCAL** whispers **HARMAN Senior**.

HARMAN Senior
Do with Beamont as you please, so Towerson die.

FISCAL
You'll not confess yet, captain?

TOWERSON
Hangman, no;
I would have don't before, if e'er I would:
To do it when my friend has suffered this,
Were to be less than he.

FISCAL
Free him.

[They free **BEAMONT**.

Beamont, I have not sworn you should not suffer.
But that you should not die; thank Julia for it.
But on your life do not delay this hour
To post from hence! so to your next plantation;
I cannot suffer a loved rival near me.

BEAMONT
I almost question if I will receive
My life from thee: 'Tis like a cure from witches;
'Twill leave a sin behind it.

FISCAL
Nay, I'm not lavish of my courtesy;
I can on easy terms resume my gift.

HARMAN Senior
Captain, you're a dead man; I'll spare your torture for your quality; prepare for execution instantly.

TOWERSON
I am prepared.

FISCAL
You die in charity, I hope?

TOWERSON

I can forgive even thee:
My innocence I need not name, you know it.
One farewell kiss of my dear Isabinda,
And all my business here on earth is done.

HARMAN Senior
Call her; she's at the door.

[Exit **FISCAL**.

TOWERSON [To **BEAMONT** embracing.]
A long and last farewell! I take my death
With the more cheerfulness, because thou liv'st
Behind me: Tell my friends, I died so as
Became a Christian and a man; give to my brave
Employers of the East India company,
The last remembrance of my faithful service;
Tell them, I seal that service with my blood;
And, dying, wish to all their factories,
And all the famous merchants of our isle,
That wealth their generous industry deserves;
But dare not hope it with Dutch partnership.
Last, there's my heart, I give it in this kiss:

[Kisses him.

Do not answer me; friendship's a tender thing,
And it would ill become me now to weep.

BEAMONT
Adieu! if I would speak, I cannot—

[Exit.

[Enter **ISABINDA**.

ISABINDA
Is it permitted me to see your eyes
Once more, before eternal night shall close them?

TOWERSON
I summoned all I had of man to see you;
'Twas well the time allowed for it was short;
I could not bear it long: 'Tis dangerous,
And would divide my love 'twixt heaven and you.
I therefore part in haste; think I am going
A sudden journey, and have not the leisure
To take a ceremonious long farewell.

ISABINDA
Do you still love me?

TOWERSON
Do not suppose I do;
'Tis for your ease, since you must stay behind me,
To think I was unkind; you'll grieve the less.

HARMAN Senior
Though I suspect you joined in my son's murder,
Yet, since it is not proved, you have your life.

ISABINDA
I thank you for't, I'll make the noblest use
Of your sad gift; that is, to die unforced:
I'll make a present of my life to Towerson,
To let you see, though worthless of his love,
I would not live without him.

TOWERSON
I charge you, love my memory, but live.

HARMAN Senior
She shall be strictly guarded from that violence
She means against herself.

ISABINDA
Vain men! there are so many paths to death,
You cannot stop them all: o'er the green turf,
Where my love's laid, there will I mourning sit,
And draw no air but from the damps that rise
Out of that hallowed earth; and for my diet,
I mean my eyes alone shall feed my mouth.
Thus will I live, till he in pity rise,
And the pale shade take me in his cold arms,
And lay me kindly by him in his grave.

[Enter **COLLINS**, and then **PEREZ, JULIA** following him.

HARMAN Senior
No more; your time's now come, you must away.

COLLINS
Now, devils, you have done your worst with tortures; death's a privation of pain, but they were a continual dying.

JULIA

Farewell, my dearest! I may have many husbands,
But never one like thee.

PEREZ
As you love my soul, take hence that woman.—
My English friends, I'm not ashamed of death,
While I have you for partners; I know you innocent,
And so am I, of this pretended plot;
But I am guilty of a greater crime;
For, being married in another country,
The governor's persuasions, and my love
To that ill woman, made me leave the first,
And make this fatal choice.
I'm justly punished; for her sake I die:
The Fiscal, to enjoy her, has accused me.
There is another cause;
By his procurement I should have killed—

FISCAL
Away with him, and stop his mouth.

[He is led off.

TOWERSON
I leave thee, life, with no regret at parting;
Full of whatever thou could'st give, I rise
From thy neglected feast, and go to sleep:
Yet, on this brink of death, my eyes are opened,
And heaven has bid me prophecy to you,
The unjust contrivers of this tragic scene:—
An age is coming, when an English monarch
With blood shall pay that blood which you have shed:
To save your cities from victorious arms,
You shall invite the waves to hide your earth[1],
And, trembling, to the, tops of houses fly,
While deluges invade your lower rooms:
Then, as with waters you have swelled our bodies,
With damps of waters shall your heads be swoln:
Till, at the last, your sapped foundations fall,
And universal ruin swallows all.

[He is led out with the English; the Dutch remain.

VAN HERRING
Ay, ay, we'll venture both ourselves and children for such another pull.

1ST DUTCHMAN
Let him prophecy when his head's off.

2ND DUTCHMAN
There's ne'er a Nostradamus of them all shall fright us from our gain.

FISCAL
Now for a smooth apology, and then a fawning letter to the king of England; and our work's done.

HARMAN Senior
'Tis done as I would wish it:
Now, brethren, at my proper cost and charges,
Three days you are my guests; in which good time
We will divide their greatest wealth by lots,
While wantonly we raffle for the rest:
Then, in full rummers, and with joyful hearts,
We'll drink confusion to all English starts.

[Exeunt.

Footnote

1. During the French invasion of 1672, the Dutch were obliged to adopt the desperate defence of cutting their dykes, and inundating the country.

EPILOGUE

A poet once the Spartans led to fight,
And made them conquer in the muse's right;
So would our poet lead you on this day,
Showing your tortured fathers in his play.
To one well-born the affront is worse, and more,
When he's abused, and baffled by a boor:
With an ill grace the Dutch their mischiefs do,
They've both ill-nature and ill-manners too.
Well may they boast themselves an ancient nation,
For they were bred ere manners were in fashion;
And their new commonwealth has set them free,
Only from honour and civility.
Venetians do not more uncouthly ride[1],
Than did their lubber state mankind bestride;
Their sway became them with as ill a mien,
As their own paunches swell above their chin:
Yet is their empire no true growth, but humour,
And only two kings' touch can cure the tumour[2].
As Cato did his Afric fruits display,
So we before your eyes their Indies lay:

All loyal English will, like him, conclude,
Let Cæsar live, and Carthage be subdued[3]!

Footnotes

1. *The situation of Venice renders it impossible to bring horses into the town; accordingly, the Venetians are proverbially bad riders.*

2. *The poet alludes to the king's evil, and to the joint war of France and England against Holland.*

3. *Allusions to Cato,—who presented to the Roman Senate the rich figs of Africa, and reminded them it was but three days sail to the country which produced such excellent fruit,—were fashionable during the Dutch war. The Lord Chancellor Shaftesbury had set the example, by applying to Holland the favourite maxim of the Roman philosopher, Delenda est Carthago. When that versatile statesman afterwards fled to Holland, he petitioned to be created a burgess of Amsterdam, to ensure him against being delivered up to England. The magistrates conferred on him the freedom desired, with the memorable words, "Ab nostra Carthagine nondum deleta, salute accipe."*

John Dryden – A Short Biography

John Dryden was born on August 9th, 1631 in the village rectory of Aldwincle near Thrapston in Northamptonshire, where his maternal grandfather was Rector of All Saints Church.

Dryden was the eldest of fourteen children born to Erasmus Dryden and wife Mary Pickering, paternal grandson of Sir Erasmus Dryden, 1st Baronet (1553–1632) and wife Frances Wilkes, Puritan landowning gentry who supported the Puritan cause and Parliament.

As a boy Dryden lived in the nearby village of Titchmarsh, Northamptonshire where it is probable that he received his first education.

In 1644 he was sent to Westminster School as a King's Scholar where his headmaster was Dr. Richard Busby, a charismatic teacher but severe disciplinarian. Having recently been re-founded by Elizabeth I, Westminster now embraced a very different religious and political spirit encouraging royalism and high Anglicanism but as a humanist public school, it maintained a curriculum which trained pupils in the art of rhetoric and the presentation of arguments for both sides of a given issue. This skill would remain with Dryden and influence his later writing and thinking, as much of it displays these dialectical patterns.

His first published poem, whilst still at Westminster, was an elegy with a strong royalist flavour on the death of his schoolmate Henry, Lord Hastings from smallpox, and alludes to the execution of King Charles I, which took place on January 30th, 1649.

In 1650 Dryden was ready for University and travelled to Trinity College, Cambridge. Dryden's undergraduate years would almost certainly have followed the standard curriculum of classics, rhetoric, and mathematics.

Dryden obtained his BA in 1654, graduating top of the list for Trinity that year.

However family tragedy struck in June of the same year when Dryden's father died, leaving him some land which generated a small income, but not enough to live on.

Returning to London during The Protectorate, Dryden now obtained work with Cromwell's Secretary of State, John Thurloe. This may have been the result of influence exercised on his behalf by his cousin the Lord Chamberlain, Sir Gilbert Pickering.

At Cromwell's funeral on 23 November 1658 Dryden was in the company of the Puritan poets John Milton and Andrew Marvell. The setting was to be a sea change in English history. From Republic to Monarchy and from one set of lauded poets to what would soon become the Age of Dryden.

The start began later that year when Dryden published the first of his great poems, Heroic Stanzas (1658), a eulogy on Cromwell's death which is necessarily cautious and prudent in its emotional display.

With the Restoration of the Monarchy in 1660 Dryden celebrated in verse with Astraea Redux, an authentic royalist panegyric. In this work the interregnum is illustrated as a time of anarchy, and Charles is seen as the restorer of peace and order.

With the king now established Dryden moved quickly to place himself as the leading poet and critic of his day and transferred his allegiances to the new government.

Along with Astraea Redux, Dryden welcomed the new regime with two more panegyrics: To His Sacred Majesty: A Panegyric on his Coronation (1662) and To My Lord Chancellor (1662).

These panegyrics are occasional and written to celebrate events. Thus they are written for the nation rather than the self, but these and others put him in good standing for his eventual appointment as Poet Laureate, where a number of event poems would be required each year and speaking for the Nation and to the Nation would be the first order of duty.

These poems suggest that Dryden was looking to court a possible patron which would have given him an income and time to explore his creative ideas but no, his path instead would be to make a living in writing for publishers, not for the aristocracy, and thus ultimately for the reading public.

In November 1662 Dryden was proposed for membership in the Royal Society, and he was elected an early fellow. However, his inactivity and non payment of dues led to his expulsion in 1666.

On December 1st, 1663 Dryden married the Royalist sister of Sir Robert Howard—Lady Elizabeth Howard (died 1714). The marriage was at St. Swithin's, London, and the consent of the parents is noted on the license, though Lady Elizabeth was then about twenty-five. She was the object of some scandals, well or ill founded; it was said that Dryden had been bullied into the marriage by her brothers. A small estate in Wiltshire was settled upon them by her father. The lady's intellect and temper were apparently not good; her husband was treated as an inferior by those of her social status.

Dryden's works occasionally contain outbursts against the married state but also celebrations of the same. Little else is known of the intimate side of his marriage.

Both Dryden and his wife were warmly attached to their children. They had three sons: Charles (1666–1704), John (1668–1701), and Erasmus Henry (1669–1710). Lady Elizabeth Dryden survived her husband, but went insane soon after his death and died in 1714.

With the re-opening of the theatres after the Puritan ban, Dryden began to also write plays. His first play, The Wild Gallant, appeared in 1663 but was not successful. From 1668 on he was contracted to produce three plays a year for the King's Company, in which he became a shareholder. During the 1660s and '70s, theatrical writing was his main source of income. He led the way in Restoration comedy, his best-known works being Marriage à la Mode (1672), as well as heroic tragedy and regular tragedy, in which his greatest success was All for Love (1678). Dryden was never fully satisfied with his theatrical writings and frequently suggested that his talents were wasted on unworthy audiences.

Certainly therefore fame as a poet looked more rewarding. In 1667, around the same time his dramatic career began, he published Annus Mirabilis, a lengthy historical poem which described the English defeat of the Dutch naval fleet and the Great Fire of London in 1666. It was a modern epic in pentameter quatrains that established him as the pre-eminent poet of his generation, and was crucial in his attaining the posts of Poet Laureate (1668) and then historiographer royal (1670).

When the Great Plague of London closed the theatres in 1665 Dryden retreated to Wiltshire where he wrote Of Dramatick Poesie (1668), arguably the best of his unsystematic prefaces and essays. Dryden constantly defended his own literary practice, and Of Dramatick Poesie, the longest of his critical works, takes the form of a dialogue in which four characters—each based on a prominent contemporary, with Dryden himself as 'Neander'—debate the merits of classical, French and English drama.

He felt strongly about the relation of the poet to tradition and the creative process, and his heroic play Aureng-zebe (1675) has a prologue which denounces the use of rhyme in serious drama. His play All for Love (1678) was written in blank verse, and was to immediately follow Aureng-Zebe.

On December 18th, 1679 he was attacked in Rose Alley near his home in Covent Garden by thugs hired by fellow poet, John Wilmot, 2nd Earl of Rochester, with whom he had a long-standing conflict. Wilmot was constantly in and out of favour with the King and his own poetry was often bawdy, lewd, even obscene and made fun of the King who would often exile him from Court.

Dryden's greatest achievements were in satiric verse: the mock-heroic Mac Flecknoe, a more personal product of his Laureate years, was a lampoon circulated in manuscript and an attack on the playwright Thomas Shadwell. Dryden's main goal in the work is to "satirize Shadwell, ostensibly for his offenses against literature but more immediately we may suppose for his habitual badgering of him on the stage and in print." It is not a belittling form of satire, but rather one which makes his object great in ways which are unexpected, transferring the ridiculous into poetry. This line of satire continued with Absalom and Achitophel (1681) and The Medal (1682). Other major works from this period are the religious poems Religio Laici (1682), written from the position of a member of the Church of England; his 1683 edition of Plutarch's Lives, translated From the Greek by Several Hands in which he introduced the word biography to English readers; and The Hind and the Panther, (1687) which celebrates his conversion to Roman Catholicism.

He wrote Britannia Rediviva celebrating the birth of a son and heir to the Catholic King and Queen on June 10th, 1688. When later in the same year James II was deposed in the Glorious Revolution, Dryden's refusal to take the oaths of allegiance to the new monarchs, William and Mary, which left him out of favour at court and he had to leave his post as Poet Laureate. Thomas Shadwell, his despised rival, succeeded him. Dryden, England's greatest literary figure, was now forced to give up his public offices and live by the proceeds of his pen alone.

Dryden was an excellent translator with his own style which brought the ire of many critics. Many felt he would embellish or expand anything he felt short or curt. Dryden did not feel such expansion was a fault, arguing that as Latin is a naturally concise language it cannot be duly represented by a comparable number of words in the much larger English vocabulary. He continued with his task of translating works by Horace, Juvenal, Ovid, Lucretius, and Theocritus, a task which he found far more satisfying than writing for the stage.

In 1694 he began work on what would be his most ambitious and defining work as translator, The Works of Virgil (1697), which was published by subscription. The publication of the translation of Virgil was a national event and brought Dryden the sum of £1,400.

His final translations appeared in the volume Fables Ancient and Modern (1700), a series of episodes from Homer, Ovid, and Boccaccio, as well as modernised adaptations from Geoffrey Chaucer interspersed with Dryden's own poems. As a translator, he made great literary works in the older languages available to readers of English.

John Dryden died on May 12th, 1700, and was initially buried in St. Anne's cemetery in Soho, before being exhumed and reburied in Westminster Abbey ten days later. He was the subject of poetic eulogies, such as Luctus Brittannici: or the Tears of the British Muses; for the Death of John Dryden, Esq. (London, 1700), and The Nine Muses.

He is seen as dominating the literary life of Restoration England to such a point that the period came to be known in literary circles as the Age of Dryden. Walter Scott called him "Glorious John."

Dryden was the dominant literary figure and influence of his age. He established the heroic couplet as a standard form of English poetry by writing successful satires, religious pieces, fables, epigrams, compliments, prologues, and plays with it; he also introduced the alexandrine and triplet into the form. In his poems, translations, and criticism, he established a poetic diction appropriate to the heroic couplet—Auden referred to him as "the master of the middle style"—that was a model for his contemporaries and for much of the 18th century. The considerable loss felt by the English literary community at his death was evident in the elegies written about him. Dryden's heroic couplet went on to become the dominant poetic form of the 18th century.

What Dryden achieved in his poetry was neither the emotional excitement of the early nineteenth-century romantics nor the intellectual complexities of the metaphysicals. Although he uses formal structures such as heroic couplets, he tried to recreate the natural rhythm of speech, and he knew that different subjects need different kinds of verse. In his preface to Religio Laici he says that "the expressions of a poem designed purely for instruction ought to be plain and natural, yet majestic... The florid, elevated and figurative way is for the passions; for (these) are begotten in the soul by showing the objects out of their true proportion.... A man is to be cheated into passion, but to be reasoned into truth."

Perhaps the following illustrates Dryden and his life—"The way I have taken, is not so streight as Metaphrase, nor so loose as Paraphrase: Some things too I have omitted, and sometimes added of my own. Yet the omissions I hope, are but of Circumstances, and such as wou'd have no grace in English; and the Addition, I also hope, are easily deduc'd from Virgil's Sense. They will seem (at least I have the Vanity to think so), not struck into him, but growing out of him".

John Dryden – A Concise Bibliography

Astraea Redux, 1660
The Wild Gallant (comedy), 1663
The Indian Emperour (tragedy), 1665
Annus Mirabilis (poem), 1667
The Enchanted Island (comedy), 1667, with William D'Avenant from Shakespeare's The Tempest
Secret Love, or The Maiden Queen, 1667
An Essay of Dramatick Poesie, 1668
An Evening's Love (comedy), 1668
Tyrannick Love (tragedy), 1669
The Conquest of Granada, 1670
The Assignation, or Love in a Nunnery, 1672
Marriage à la mode, 1672
Amboyna, or the Cruelties of the Dutch to the English Merchants, 1673
The Mistaken Husband (comedy), 1674
Aureng-zebe, 1675
All for Love, 1678
Oedipus (heroic drama), 1679, an adaptation with Nathaniel Lee of Sophocles' Oedipus
Absalom and Achitophel, 1681
The Spanish Fryar, 1681
Mac Flecknoe, 1682
The Medal, 1682
Religio Laici, 1682
To the Memory of Mr. Oldham, 1684
Threnodia Augustalis, 1685
The Hind and the Panther, 1687
A Song for St. Cecilia's Day, 1687
Britannia Rediviva, 1688, written to mark the birth of a Prince of Wales.
Amphitryon, 1690
Don Sebastian (play), 1690
Creator Spirit, by whose aid, 1690. Translation of Rabanus Maurus' Veni Creator Spiritus
King Arthur, 1691
Cleomenes, 1692
The Art of Satire, 1693
Love Triumphant, 1694
The Works of Virgil, 1697
Alexander's Feast, 1697
Fables, Ancient and Modern, 1700

www.ingramcontent.com/pod-product-compliance
Lightning Source LLC
Chambersburg PA
CBHW061503040426
42450CB00008B/1466